FINANCE FOR SPORT AND LEISURE MANAGERS

Today's sport and leisure managers need to understand the financial side of the industry in order to offer the most cost-effective facilities and to make sound business decisions. However, to the non-accountant, the language and practice of finance can seem bewildering and impenetrable.

Finance for Sport and Leisure Managers: An Introduction introduces the core concepts and rewards of good financial management, and guides students clearly through the seeming maze of financial terms and processes. Throughout the text financial theory, regulations and practice are set out alongside worked examples drawn from sport and leisure contexts.

Designed for students with no prior knowledge of financial reporting, this book enables students to build understanding and confidence. The text includes:

- Industry specific case studies
- The 'mechanics' of financial accounting
- Income statements and balance sheets
- Why cash is not the same as profit
- How to analyse and interpret financial statements
- Self-tests to check and confirm your understanding.

Written by experts in accounting and sport management, this unique textbook is ideal for sport and leisure management students as well as for practising managers looking for a quick-reference guide to everyday financial questions.

Robert Wilson is a Senior Lecturer in Sport Management in the Faculty of Health and Wellbeing, Sheffield Hallam University. His subject specialisms are financial reporting and management accounting and his main research interest is the economics and finance of sport and leisure. He is a recognised expert in learning, teaching and assessment in Higher Education.

John Joyce is the Professional Courses Leader in the Faculty of Organisation and Management at Sheffield Hallam University. His subject specialism is financial decision making and his main research interest is accounting education. He is a recognised expert in the educational systems of professional accounting.

FINANCE FOR SPORT AND LEISURE MANAGERS

An Introduction

ROBERT WILSON AND JOHN JOYCE

Routledge
Taylor & Francis Group

LONDON AND NEW YORK

First published 2008
by Routledge
2 Park Square, Milton Park, Abingdon, Oxon OX14 4RN

Simultaneously published in the USA and Canada
by Routledge
270 Madison Ave, New York, NY 10016

Routledge is an imprint of the Taylor & Francis Group, an informa business

© 2008 Robert Wilson and John Joyce

Designed and typeset in Zapf Humanist and Eras
by Keystroke, 28 High Street, Tettenhall, Wolverhampton
Printed and bound in Great Britain
by TJ International Ltd, Padstow, Cornwall

British Library Cataloguing in Publication Data
A catalogue record for this book is available from the British Library

Library of Congress Cataloging in Publication Data
Wilson, Robert 1980–
Finance for sport and leisure managers : an introduction / Robert Wilson and John Joyce.
p. cm.
ISBN 978–0–415–40446–4 (hardcover) — ISBN 978–0–415–40447–1 (softcover)
1. Sports—Accounting. 2. Sports—Finance. 3. Leisure industry—Accounting.
I. Joyce, John, 1955– II. Title.
GV716.W55 2007
796.06′91—dc22
2007013244

ISBN10: 0–415–40447–9 (pbk)
ISBN10: 0–415–40446–0 (hbk)
ISBN10: 0–203–93442–3 (ebk)

ISBN13: 978–0–415–40447–1 (pbk)
ISBN13: 978–0–415–40446–4 (hbk)
ISBN13: 978–0–203–93442–5 (ebk)

CONTENTS

PART 1 THE BASICS   1

V

vi

LIST OF FIGURES

LIST OF TABLES

PREFACE

This book has been written because we like students and we like helping them. We thought one way to help students, even those we never see, would be to write a book to help them understand 'finance'. It's not that we think all other books are bad or that our book is better. It is that we think that our book is different. We have tried not to let the book become yet another finance/accounting text that gets bogged down with terminology and formulas to remember. We have tried to make the book student friendly and as such have written it in a less than formal style. We hope you enjoy it and that it offers an alternative to the mountains of academic texts that, in many cases, seem only to make accounting appear difficult.

Finance for Sport and Leisure Managers: An Introduction provides a practical, applied and critical look at the important, but often confusing, area of public, private and voluntary sector sport and leisure finance. This book is specifically aimed at students with no prior knowledge of financial reporting and seeks to offer a 'one stop shop' to understanding the bewildering language of finance in a sport and leisure context. By adopting a step-by-step approach you will be guided through the maze of financial rules, regulations, concepts and terminology so that you will understand their meaning and application in the context of the sport and leisure industry.

The sport and leisure industry has changed at a startling pace. The Sport Industry Research Centre (Sport Market Forecasts 2005–2009) suggests that sport accounts for 2.5 per cent of consumer expenditure. In 2004 this equated to about £18.7 billion. We can probably rest our case for the importance of this book here. As a future (or current) sport and leisure manager you need to get a piece of this huge cake. Once you get it, you need to control it and use it so that you can be effective in your job. You should therefore find this book a useful resource text. You can use it while studying financial accounting on a degree programme or put it on the shelf and dip into it as and when you need to during your career. We think that one of the really helpful aspects of this book is the use of examples throughout the chapters and the activities that we ask you to complete. Very often you might need to look at some figures and could have no idea what they mean; we'll give you the knowledge, show you how to use that knowledge and, more importantly, the understanding to be able to explain what it means.

The book is structured to present logical sequencing of material. Conceptually the book is divided into three main sections to help you to engage with the subject gradually. To start your journey down the road to financial understanding we first deal with the context of sport and leisure and the concepts and rules of accounting (The Basics). Then we show you The Mechanics and the logic of accounting transactions that lead to the compilation of financial statements. Finally we show you how to analyse the financial statements of organisations: this needs knowledge, understanding and application of accounting and accounting terminology (The Meaning).

You'll find an introduction at the beginning of each of the eight chapters that summarises what they are about and how you will be taken through them. This is a progressive book so we will build on the skills that you have grasped throughout. When you have worked through these chapters you will be able to construct basic accounts and more importantly you will be able to analyse and discuss what the figures actually mean. The emphasis throughout the book is on the application of key principles. As such you can work through the book at your own pace, examine some of the issues in depth and see how everything works in practice through the use of industry examples and case studies. You'll also find some review questions at the end of each chapter that you can work through and continue to apply your knowledge to.

We recognise that most of you will not have studied accounting or finance before. Consequently you will find that we have tried to write this book in a clear, concise and user-friendly style. We will not take you down blind alleys to explain the meaning of obscure transactions and events. Instead we will stick to the rules and principles that will be of benefit to you on a day-to-day basis. Where the use of some terminology is unavoidable we provide clear explanations and supporting examples where necessary. In addition all of the key terms are listed in alphabetical order in the glossary at the back of the book.

Interspersed through most of the chapters are a number of activities. We strongly advise you to complete these questions. They are designed to stimulate the sort of quick fire questions that we, as lecturers, would fire at you in a classroom and give you an opportunity to check that you understand what has been covered so far.

Welcome to the book.

Rob and John

PART 1
THE BASICS

CHAPTER ONE

FINANCIAL ACCOUNTING IN CONTEXT

On completion of this chapter you will be able to:

- Communicate the purpose of accounting in a sport and leisure context.
- Identify and describe the users of accounting information.
- Distinguish between financial and management accounts.
- Understand the information needs of user groups.
- Understand the statutory requirements of sport and leisure organisations.

INTRODUCTION

Let's get this straight. Accounting is *not* just about numbers. You *do not* have to be a skilled mathematician to understand a set of accounts and you *do not* have to spend hours of time learning various theories. Instead you can appreciate the need for accounts and how to work with accounts (and accountants!) by understanding the 'rules' and procedures that accountants follow. Put simply, accounting is a way of showing to external stakeholders and internal management how well a business has performed over a period of time and its prospects for continuing to operate.

The aim of this book is to focus on how to use accounts, not produce them. As future managers you need to be able to interpret and then communicate the meaning of accounts to a variety of people for a variety of reasons. The identification of the users of the accounts and their needs provides the reasons for the accounts. Without an understanding of why the accounts are being prepared, the numbers and the situation they portray will be meaningless. This chapter aims to identify the user groups and their needs and illustrate why financial accounting is integral to the sport and leisure industry.

You may have heard the terms 'accounting statements' or 'set of accounts' but do you understand what they actually mean? You may also have wondered who uses accounting information and what the purpose of accounting actually is. We will therefore start with a quick overview to help you understand what accounting is all about.

KEY TERMS

ACCOUNTING

This is about identifying, collecting, measuring, recording, summarising and communicating financial information.

ACCOUNT

A record that is kept as part of an accounting system. It will be a record of the transactions and will be recorded in monetary values.

FINANCIAL STATEMENTS

The complete set of accounts. This will include the balance sheet (this shows the organisation's assets and liabilities), income statement (the profit and loss account) and the cash flow statement. Also included will be notes on the accounting policies used and significant activities.

ACCOUNTING IN SPORT AND LEISURE

Organisations, ranging from huge multi-million pound operations, such as Manchester United Football Club, to small voluntary sports clubs and teams, such as a local swimming club, will produce financial statements at least once a year. The objective of the final accounts is to provide information to a range of users (not just the owner or shareholders). The information provided in the accounts is concerned with the resources held by the business and how they are used. The accounts therefore show the organisation's position at the end of a financial period, an analysis of changes during the period, and point to the future prospects of the business. This information will be of great importance to anyone who has an interest in the business because it shows whether or not the organisation is achieving its goals.

At this point it is probably worth you having a look at a set of financial statements. If nothing else this will show you the financial results of an organisation and how the accountant presents them. In Figures 1.1, 1.2 and 1.3 you will find a paragraph or two about the organisation's goals, the profit and loss account and balance sheet for Southampton Leisure Holdings, that is the group that owns and operates Southampton Football Club, for the period ending 30 June 2006. These are actual excerpts from the company's annual report and something that we may ask you to think about later. It is important that you don't worry about what everything means here but it is useful if you can see what the two statements are basically illustrating while referring to the corporate statement.

CORPORATE STATEMENT

TO STRIVE IN PARTNERSHIP WITH THE CLUB'S SUPPORTERS, SHAREHOLDERS, POTENTIAL NEW INVESTORS, SPONSORS, EMPLOYEES AND OTHER STAKEHOLDERS, INCLUDING THE LOCAL COMMUNITY, TO RE-ESTABLISH AND MAINTAIN SOUTHAMPTON FOOTBALL CLUB AS A FINANCIALLY ROBUST BUSINESS. A BUSINESS WHOSE PRINCIPAL ASSET IS A STYLISH AND ENTERTAINING FOOTBALL TEAM THAT EVOKES LOYALTY, PRIDE AND PASSION ON THE PART OF ITS FOLLOWERS. A TEAM THAT IS GENUINELY CAPABLE OF FINISHING AMONGST THE TOP TEN CLUBS WITHIN THE FA PREMIER LEAGUE AND REACHING THE LATTER STAGES OF THE FA AND LEAGUE CUP COMPETITIONS EVERY SEASON.

Figure 1.1 Southampton Football Club Corporate Statement

Source: From Southampton Leisure Holdings Plc Annual Report and Accounts 2006.

For the information that you have on Southampton Football Club (see this and following pages) can you answer the following questions?

- Is the organisation meeting its corporate statement?
- How has the business performed over the past year?
- What are its future prospects?

5

CONSOLIDATED PROFIT AND LOSS ACCOUNT
PERIOD ENDED 30 JUNE 2006

	Note	Operations excluding player trading 2006 £'000	Player trading* 2006 £'000	13 months ended 30 June 2006 £'000	12 months ended 31 May 2005 £'000
TURNOVER	1	**25,696**	–	**25,696**	44,828
Cost of sales	2	**(26,055)**	**(5,308)**	**(31,363)**	(44,990)
Gross loss	2	**(359)**	**(5,308)**	**(5,667)**	(162)
Administrative expenses		**(6,861)**	–	**(6,861)**	(6,324)
OPERATING LOSS	3	**(7,220)**	**(5,308)**	**(12,528)**	(6,486)
Profit on disposal of players		–	**11,241**	**11,241**	5,602
Profit on sale of tangible fixed assets	4	–	–	–	3,094
(Loss)/profit before interest and taxation		**(7,220)**	**5,933**	**(1,287)**	2,210
Net interest payable	5			**(2,008)**	(1,978)
(LOSS)/PROFIT ON ORDINARY ACTIVITIES BEFORE TAXATION				**(3,295)**	232
Tax on (loss)/profit on ordinary activities	8			**953**	(159)
(LOSS)/PROFIT ON ORDINARY ACTIVITIES AFTER TAXATION				**(2,342)**	73
BASIC (LOSS)/EARNINGS PER SHARE	10			**(8.34)p**	0.26p
DILUTED (LOSS)/EARNINGS PER SHARE	10			**(8.34)p**	0.26p

*player trading represents the amortisation of registrations and the profit or loss on disposal of registrations.

All amounts derive from continuing activities.

There are no recognised gains or losses for the current financial period and preceding financial year other than as stated in the profit and loss account. Accordingly, a statement of total recognised gains and losses has not been presented.

There is no material difference between the results reported above and the results on an unmodified historical cost bais. Accordingly, a note of historical cost profits and losses has not been presented.

Figure 1.2 Southampton Football Club Profit and Loss Account

Source: From Southampton Leisure Holdings Plc Annual Report and Accounts 2006.

It is difficult to confidently say what is really going on, as we have no knowledge of what all of the terms mean on both the profit and loss (P&L) and balance sheet (B/S) – in fact unless you have cheated and looked ahead you probably don't even know what the P&L and B/S are! Don't worry, if we apply a bit of logic we can actually see through the financial maze and work up some answers.

The answers to the questions will be interlinked. The P&L tells us that the football club has made a loss of £2.3m so we can assume that it is not yet a 'financially robust business'. Moreover, if we look at the figures for 2005 we can be a little more forthright with our answer. The company reported a profit of £73,000 and this indicates that things have actually become worse in terms of financial performance. The general implications of this will be that the club has less flexibility to buy new players and could therefore struggle to

CONSOLIDATED AND COMPANY BALANCE SHEETS
AT 30 JUNE 2006

		Group		Company	
		30 JUNE 2006	31 May 2005	**As restated 30 June 2006**	As restated 31 May 2005
	Note	**£'000**	£'000	**£'000**	£'000
FIXED ASSETS					
Intangible assets	11	**3,757**	13,255	–	–
Tangible assets	12	**35,866**	36,164	**4,065**	2,437
Investments	13	**–**	–	**10,191**	10,191
		39,623	49,419	**14,256**	12,628
CURRENT ASSETS					
Stocks	14	**404**	391	**–**	–
Debtors	15	**6,466**	6,239	**9,257**	8,449
Investments	16	**2,480**	2,480	**–**	–
Cash at bank and in hand		**2,220**	2,012	**437**	298
		11,570	11,122	**9,694**	8,747
CREDITORS: AMOUNTS FALLING DUE WITHIN ONE YEAR	17	**(11,294)**	(17,079)	**(6,439)**	(3,455)
NET CURRENT ASSETS/(LIABILITIES)	0	**276**	(5,957)	**3,255**	5,292
TOTAL ASSETS LESS CURRENT LIABILITIES		**39,899**	43,462	**17,511**	17,920
CREDITORS: AMOUNTS FALLING DUE AFTER MORE THAN ONE YEAR	18	**(28,555)**	(29,094)	**–**	–
PROVISIONS	20	**(2,590)**	(3,132)	**–**	–
NET ASSETS	0	**8,754**	11,236	**17,511**	17,920
CAPITAL AND RESERVES					
Share capital	21	**1,405**	1,405	**1,405**	1,405
Share premium account	22	**3,340**	3,340	**3,340**	3,340
Other reserves	22	**1,050**	1,050	**7,560**	7,560
Profit and loss account	22	**2,959**	5,441	**5,206**	5,615
SHAREHOLDERS' FUNDS	23	**8,754**	11,236	**17,511**	17,920

These financial statements were approved by the Boad of Directors and authorised for issue on 29 September 2006.

Figure 1.3 Southampton Football Club Balance Sheet

Source: From Southampton Leisure Holdings Plc Annual Report and Accounts 2006.

meet some of its other aspirations such as 'entertaining football' and 'finishing in the top 10 in the FA Premier League' (see Figure 1.1). The B/S tells us what things the business has to use so although the business has not made a profit this year it can cover all of its debts (total creditors) with the things that it owns (total assets). On the whole it is not too bad a picture given the nature of the football industry.

Hopefully what this exercise will show you is that with a little bit of thought and guidance you can understand financial statements. Once you have the skills you will be able to see through the maze! However, it is crucial that you realise that no single statement can give the whole picture: profit and cash are both important indicators but they are very, very different. For any business, the ability to pay its debts as they fall due is vital to the success or failure of the organisation: cash can be used to pay the bills but profit cannot.

THE IMPORTANCE OF FINANCE IN SPORT AND LEISURE

Many organisations borrow to fund their expansion plans. In fact such borrowing could be essential to acquire the resources needed to become or continue to be competitive. Borrowing is based on the assumption that future returns will be big enough to cover the loan (and the interest!). However, problems will occur if the business fails to meet its obligations to the people it owes money to by not generating earnings big enough to cover its responsibilities. It might seem obvious but it is a fact that accurate statements and forecasts about the current state of the business and its future cash flows are needed. Businesses need financial information to make decisions; although sometimes even with this information the wrong decisions can be made. This is a lesson that one football club learnt the hard way (and others continue to learn).

Football is business and big business at that. Over the last 10 years general interest in the game has increased, as have amounts of investment, income from television broadcast rights, and corporate sponsorship. For example BskyB paid over £600m to Premier League football clubs between 1997 and 2001 for television rights. The contract for the current period (2003–2007) is £1.024 billion.

In addition to television income, success in European competition, in particular the UEFA Champions League (UCL) has offered significant rewards to many of the top teams. The winners of the UCL are estimated to earn up to £20m. With such large sources of cash available to the top teams, a winning team is essential. Only the top four clubs from the Premier League qualify to play in the UCL the following season. Consequently the UCL is not a guaranteed source of income: teams need to perform well to earn their place and the associated cash rewards. On the downside, if a team performs badly there are also cash implications: sources of income will dry up.

Despite the growth in potential financial gains the sport of football has been blighted by a series of high profile problems. It is thought that only one in four football clubs expects to make a profit. This is mainly because of high transfer fees and the high wages that are paid to attract players in to try to build successful teams. At the time of writing Sheffield United Football Club had just published its financial statements for the season in which it won promotion to the English Premier League (EPL): the club reported a loss of £9.6m, and although it hopes to recoup this through the new funding streams available in the EPL, it is clear that a game that has been perceived as cash rich is not so. There is no better way to show this than reflecting on what happened to Leeds United Football Club.

FINANCE, FOOTBALL AND LEEDS UNITED FC

At the beginning of 2000 the Chairman of the club was determined to bring back the glory days to Elland Road. The board of directors supported his ambitions and in retrospect it is easy to see why they did so. Financially Leeds seemed healthy and they were operating in a buoyant industry. Leeds had made an operating profit and things looked good: gate receipts were up by around 20 per cent on the previous season, TV revenues were up by 40 per cent and merchandising activity was up about 15 per cent.

The Chairman thought that with the right players Leeds stood a great chance of challenging Manchester United for the Premiership crown and getting into the UCL on a more regular basis and therefore benefiting from the associated incomes. So out he went and spent £15m. Does this figure sound a lot? Perhaps not when you consider what some clubs were spending. However if we look at the figure another way we can see why the club began to get in trouble. The club's turnover in the 1998–1999 season, that is money that it earned before any bills had been paid, came to £37m. The money spent on transfers the following season was about 40 per cent of that and needed to be funded from external sources.

The only way that banks and other lenders will offer credit facilities is by securing the loan against some of the business assets. In the case of Leeds this meant that the stadium, training facilities and even players were used to provide security to its financial backers. This may sound a little radical but for Leeds it looked to be a risk worth taking. They reached the semi-final of the UEFA Cup and finished third in the EPL which gained them a place in the qualifying stages of the UCL. The financial statements reflected the successful season: TV revenue was up 56 per cent and gate receipts up by around 33 per cent and consequently turnover jumped from £37m to £57m.

In light of this success the Board of Directors at Leeds decided to continue with their strategies and purchased some new players for the next season. In total around £18m was spent on players, including Olivier Dacourt and Mark Viduka. After a shaky start the team progressed to the group stages of the UCL and occupied sixth place in the EPL. The board decided to strengthen further and bought Rio Ferdinand for £18.6m (and set a new record for a British transfer fee). Then things started to get difficult! Creditors got a little edgy: they were worried about the amount of money that Leeds owed. Leeds did try to restructure its financing but the potential for raising more finance was exhausted. The only way to pay off the growing debts was to achieve the Chairman's dream and go all the way in the UCL and EPL. An honourable defeat against Valencia in the semi-final of the European Cup relieved the pressure by £20m but the debt problems were still there. Liabilities started to increase and the club struggled to meet its interest payments. Although income may fluctuate, operating expenses do not move with it. For example, the players were on high wages and expected to be paid even when they lost! The wage bill grew by around £12m. Leeds reported losses of £9m in 1999, £21m in 2000 and £31m in 2001.

At the start of the next season they spent again (still chasing the dream): £11m on Robbie Keane, £7m for Seth Johnson and £11m for Robbie Fowler. The strategy looked to have worked: Leeds went top of the EPL on New Year's Day. However, by March Leeds was 10 points adrift and was unlikely to qualify for the UCL. Net debt reached £82m, and interest payments were around £1m per month. With no prospects for continued success, and more importantly the associated high incomes, the financial backers began to worry (they lent money to Leeds as a business proposition, not because they were football fans!). Leeds was in serious trouble and needed a new strategy.

The club needed to generate cash from something other than football: it decided to sell off some of its assets. In theory this was a reasonable idea, however in practice the players that were sold did not reach their market potential. Players such as Harry Kewel and Robbie Fowler were sold for less than half of their true market price. Consequently, Leeds did not generate enough cash and could not cover its debts. The rest as they say is history.

It was reported in 2006 that the club had finally paid the last of its creditors and was now in a position to re-build. However by 2006 the damage was clear to see: Leeds is no longer in the EPL and is struggling to come to terms with life in the Coca-Cola Championship.

This case study provides a good example of how trying to grow by borrowing vast sums of money without sustainable sources of income can destabilise any business. Cast your mind back to the paragraph at the end of the previous Activity where we made the point about business failure by not paying debts as they fall due. This rule is fundamental in business and a lesson that you need to understand before you can successfully manage any organisation.

Questions

1   Do you think that the Leeds United model suggests that football clubs, or any sport organisation, should avoid borrowing?
2   Do you think that there is a right level of borrowing and if so how do you think that it could be calculated?
3   The strategy to buy players was the Chairman's idea but what other things could Leeds have done to improve on-the-field success?

Borrowing is not necessarily a bad thing – nor for that matter is debt. The main issue is being able to service the debt. Can you afford to pay your credit card bill? If so you can service your borrowing and reduce your debt. If not your debt will grow in much the same way as it did for Leeds United. The answer to the first question in the case study could therefore be 'No, providing that the clubs and organisations do not borrow more than they can afford to service'.

In much the same way we can answer the second question. The right level of borrowing for any club will be determined by the amounts they can afford to pay back. Think about how a personal mortgage is worked out. If you wanted a mortgage of £100,000 costing £500 per month you would expect to have earning power of at least £1,000 per month. This would allow you to pay for the mortgage without getting into difficulty. On the other hand if you only had an earning potential of £600 per month you would struggle to have a life and pay your mortgage. It is the same in sport except on a much larger scale. Leeds United did not have enough money coming in to pay for its high level borrowing.

The final question is a little trickier. Short of buying better players (which would have cost more) how could the club have improved on-the-field success? Perhaps by getting a better manager? They tried that two or three times without any joy. Performance related pay? This may have worked to motivate players more but they were already tied to contracts. We think the simple answer is 'who knows?'. In hindsight it is easy to say that Leeds United got it wrong. If the financial packages had been sorted out more effectively then things may not have gone so wildly out of control. Hopefully this book will help you to spot the similar problems in your working life before it is too late and prevent you from getting into the position that Leeds United was in!

USER GROUPS

Financial information is relevant to a range of users and for a variety of reasons. Before we go on to show who these users are and why they need accounting information why not try the following activity?

ACTIVITY

State a business, organisation or club and then make a list of who you think will be interested in its financial information. Also state why you think they need the information. (Give yourself 5 minutes to complete this activity.)

Your ideas will generally depend on the type of business that you were thinking about. For example, if you were thinking about Gloucester Rugby Football Club you could have identified Tom Walkinshaw as a user of information because he will want to see how his company (Gloucester Rugby Football Club Limited) is performing, for example did he make a profit last year? Alternatively if you were thinking about your local athletics club you could have identified one of the club's members because they would want to see how the club was using their subscriptions.

Clubs and associations exist to provide services to their members. They must therefore ensure that the money received through subscriptions and fund raising is sufficient to cover their running costs. However, businesses exist to make profits for their owners.

Generally, information relating to the finances of a business is of interest to its owners, managers, trade contacts (e.g. suppliers), providers of finance (e.g. banks), employees and customers. These people will want to see the strengths and future prospects of the business. Let's see how you got on with the activity. Highlighted below is our list of users and some insights into why these people use the information. Does your list match ours?

User Groups	Areas of interest
Owners of a company	These people will want to know how well the management is doing on a day-to-day basis and how much profit they can take from the business for their own use.
Managers	Need the financial information so that they can make future plans for the business and see how well their decisions have been.
Trade contacts (i.e. suppliers)	Suppliers will want to know if they are going to be paid on time by the business.
Providers of finance (i.e. banks)	Lenders will want to make sure that any loans and interest payments are going to be made on time.
Her Majesty's Revenue and Customs (HMRC)	Needs information about the profits of the business so that they can work out how much tax the business owes. Also needs details for VAT and employees' income tax.
Employees	May want to know whether their jobs are safe and that they are going to be paid.
Customers	Will want to know if goods/services purchased are going to be delivered/provided. These people may also be interested in investing in the company and therefore will want to know whether it is a good prospect.

It is widely acknowledged that the financial statements cannot meet the needs of all its potential user groups. However, most users will have common requirements: the organisation's ability to make a profit or loss, how much cash it has (this is called 'liquidity') and its ability to fulfil obligations to clients.

Accessibility by the general public to financial information will depend on the 'status' of the specific organisation in which they are interested. For example, the sports wear company Kitlocker (a case study that we will look at later) is presently operating as a partnership. As a result the owners are not required to make any sort of public disclosure of financial information. The main users of their information will be the owners themselves and any managers they appoint. However, a company that is listed on the London Stock Exchange, such as Powerleague (5-a-side football league operators), has a statutory obligation to publish an annual report (which will include its financial statements) and to send copies to its shareholders and Companies House.

LEGAL IDENTITY

It is important to realise that in accounting, the business and the owners are seen as two separate bodies. You can see this in the balance sheet for Southampton Football Club (see Figure 1.4): 'capital' is the owner's stake in the business and the accounts clearly show this.

CAPITAL AND RESERVES			
Share capital	21	**1,405**	1,405
Share premium account	22	**3,340**	3,340
Other reserves	22	**1,050**	1,050
Profit and loss account	22	**2,959**	5,441
SHAREHOLDERS' FUNDS	23	**8,754**	11,236

Figure 1.4 Southampton Football Club Capital

Source: From Southampton Leisure Holdings Plc Annual Report and Accounts 2006.

This concept is always applied in accounting. In law the business and the owners can be separate. The law recognises that a business may acquire assets and debts in its own right. In such a situation, if the business goes bankrupt the shareholders are not required to pay the deficit: the debts are the responsibility of the business. The owners (shareholders) have limited liability.

Before we look at the different types of business you need to understand that they can take two forms: unincorporated and incorporated. Unincorporated businesses are sole traders or partnerships. Incorporated businesses are public or private companies.

LIMITED LIABILITY

Legal protection given to the owners of a company. When a company cannot pay its debts the shareholders will not be liable to contribute more than their initial investment towards the overall debt.

UNLIMITED LIABILITY

In short, the opposite of limited liability. At least one of the shareholders (be it a sole trader or partnership) will be liable for the total debt their company incurs.

LIQUIDATION

This is quite simply the process by which a company ceases to exist. It is a legal status rather than a financial position.

Sole traders: one person owns the business. In this case there is no legal separation of identity between the business and the owner (although there will be for accounting purposes). The debts of the business are also the debts of the owner and there is no obligation for the public disclosure of financial information about the business.

Partnerships: this is when two or more people enter into business together. The liability will be shared between the owners and at least one of them will have unlimited liability for the debts they may incur.

Private company (Limited company): this is a company where the obligation of its owners is limited to the amount that they invested. If the business goes bankrupt the owners will lose their shares but the creditors cannot chase them for the company's debts. To form a limited company it must be registered at Companies House and the firm must have various legal documents including a Memorandum and Articles of Association. There need only be one director. The company must prepare annual accounts and submit them to Companies House. Private limited companies may be a small family based business or they could be a major international organisation (such as the Virgin group).

Public company: a public limited company (plc) has shares, but the key difference between private and public companies is that the shares in a public company can be purchased by anyone (they are traded on the stock exchange). Ownership is therefore open to any-one who wants to buy shares. Plcs have legal requirements in that they have to produce

14

annual reports and accounts and file them with Companies House. They must have two directors.

FINANCIAL VERSUS MANAGEMENT ACCOUNTS

We now know that many different people use accounting information and we will shortly look further into what their information needs are. However, we can already see that accounting information can look both forwards (i.e. to the future) and backwards (i.e. to the past) and that there are people both inside and outside the business who use it. In a nutshell financial accounting (what we are predominantly interested in for this book) concerns the preparation of information for external use, and is mainly concerned with reporting on past events. On the other hand management accounting is (as the name implies!) about providing information that is primarily focused on the needs of management and will therefore additionally look to the future and will cover planning and control aspects. Management accounting is not a statutory requirement.

This book will focus on financial accounting and how to use the information to form a view on how well a business has performed.

STATUTORY REQUIREMENTS IN SPORT AND LEISURE

Each and every sport organisation has a responsibility to produce financial statements: the legal requirements will be determined by the nature of the company, i.e. whether it is a sole trader or a public company as we discussed earlier. Later in the book you will find out how these statements are developed and how to interpret them. However, to end this chapter we will briefly examine the meaning of the two main financial statements that will be drawn up by financial accountants: the balance sheet and profit and loss account (illustrated earlier in this chapter when we looked at Southampton Football Club). You should, however, note that what was once called the 'profit and loss account' is now referred to in International Accounting Standards as the 'income statement' (we will use the terms interchangeably because at the time of writing the shift was just beginning).

KEY TERMS

BALANCE SHEET

The **balance sheet** is a list of all of the assets owned by a business and all of the liabilities owed by a business at a specific point in time. It is often referred to as a 'snapshot' of the financial position of the business at a specific moment in time (normally the end of the financial year).

It is worth mentioning here that 'assets' are resources that the business owns, for example buildings, machinery and vehicles. Such resources will be used by the business in its operations. There may also be bank balances and cash. These will hold the funds that the business needs to operate. However, the business may also owe money to its owners, other people or organisations – we call these liabilities. Why not skip back a few pages and have a look at the assets and liabilities for Southampton Football Club and familiarise yourself with what they own and owe?

PROFIT AND LOSS ACCOUNT

The **profit and loss account** (income statement) is a statement showing the profits (or losses) recognised during a period. The profit is calculated by deducting expenditure (including charges for capital maintenance) from income.

A limited company will produce a profit and loss account for the period of one year. However, it is not uncommon for internal users to produce profit and loss accounts on a quarterly or even monthly basis. Profit and loss accounts that you come across are likely to be in annual reports and will therefore be for a 12-month period. Organisations that are 'not-for-profit' such as charities produce a similar statement called an income and expenditure account, which will show any surplus of income over expenditure (or a deficit if expenditure exceeds income). Again go back to the statements for Southampton Football Club and see what is going on there.

SUMMARY

This first chapter has been designed to introduce you to financial accounting. During the chapter we have shown you why financial accounting is important to sport and leisure organisations and have also highlighted the main users of financial information. Furthermore, you have been introduced to the main financial statements – you will learn how to understand and construct these during the remainder of this book. Although we will come back to visit these in much more detail later on it was worth letting you see what the end result of this book will be. You should by now have grasped a few of the basic skills required to read the financial statements and should be able to see why the information is so valuable to businesses and why it should be so important to you as you embark on a journey to understand finance in sport and leisure.

Earlier you examined some information about Southampton Football Club. This book focuses on Sport and Leisure so it is useful to have a look at a leisure organisation here.

Arena Leisure plc stages 25 per cent of all horse racing in the United Kingdom. It owns, runs and manages a portfolio of racecourses to provide a solid base for the future development of the group. It maintains a continued focus on improving its fixture list which includes 75 race meetings at Southwell, 23 race meetings at Folkestone, 90 race meetings at Lingfield Park, 27 race meetings at Royal Windsor, 21 race meetings at Worcester and 97 race meetings at Wolverhampton. In addition it aims to increase overall attendances at its courses, currently around 750,000 people a year, and expand its non-racing facilities such as gambling, sport and leisure clubs and television.

To answer the following questions you need to go online and download its annual report. It can be found at www.arenaleisureplc.com.

Questions

▓ Is the organisation meeting its corporate statement?
▓ How has the business performed over the past year?
▓ What are its future prospects?

QUESTIONS FOR REVIEW

1 Why do managers use financial information?
2 List three users of financial information (ignoring managers).
3 What are the four main company types?
4 What type of information does financial accounting examine?
5 True or False: The balance sheet helps us determine the profit of an organisation?

17

1   Managers use financial information to make decisions and to evaluate the success of such decisions.

2   You could have suggested any three from the following list:

- Owners of a company
- Trade contacts
- Providers of finance
- Her Majesty's Revenue and Customs
- Employees
- Customers.

3   Types of businesses are: sole traders, partnerships, private company and public company. They can also be 'for profit' and 'not-for-profit' organisations.

4   Financial accounting examines 'historical information'.

5   False: The balance sheet shows what assets the company owns and what liabilities it has. The profit and loss account (income statement) reports the profit (or loss) made by the company.

18

CHAPTER TWO

THE 'RULES' OF FINANCIAL ACCOUNTING

On completion of this chapter you will be able to:

- Understand accounting concepts, bases and policies.
- Use the main financial accounting terminology.
- Identify the key regulations for financial accountants.

INTRODUCTION

Although the aim of this book is not to teach you how to become an accountant, we do need to show you how to use and read accounts. Consequently you need an understanding of how accounts are prepared (otherwise the numbers will be relatively meaningless!). Therefore the next four chapters will explain the guiding rules and principles and illustrate how accountants use them to construct the accounts. This will give you the necessary skills to prepare basic accounts should your course or employer require you to do so. This chapter will explain the concepts, statements and guidelines that form the 'rules' of financial accounting.

In Chapter 1 you learnt that accounting is about identifying, collecting, measuring, recording, summarising and communicating financial information. The information has a purpose – it is to satisfy the needs of users, i.e. the information will be used. Consequently it must be fit for the purpose.

When you had a look at the financial statements of Southampton Football Club and Arena Leisure you will have noticed that they contained a great deal of information. Hopefully, you will have also noticed that much of the terminology and layouts were very similar. This is because both companies have to conform to the regulatory framework of accounting. To reinforce the point have a look at the excerpts from the Rugby Football Union (RFU) in Figure 2.1. For those of you that don't know, the RFU is the governing body for all rugby played in England.

Group profit and loss account

for the year to 30 June 2006

	Notes	2006 £m	2005 restated £m
Revenue			
Ticket income		14.4	17.6
Broadcasting		19.6	16.1
Sponsorship		13.9	12.3
Hospitality & catering		21.6	25.5
Merchandising & licensing		5.9	8.4
Travel and leisure		0.5	–
Other income		6.8	6.7
		82.7	86.6
Costs			
Direct		18.7	22.7
Elite rugy		13.0	11.3
Community rugby		14.1	11.2
Business & administration		13.5	11.1
Stadium		7.2	7.0
		66.5	63.3
Operating profit	2	16.2	23.3
Alllocations to clubs and Constituent Bodies		(19.6)	(18.9)
Share of losses from associated undertakings		(0.1)	–
Interest receivable net	4	1.8)	2.0
(Loss) profit on ordinary activities before taxation		(1.7)	6.4
Taxation credit (charge) on ordinary activities	5	0.5	(2.8)
(Loss) profit on ordinary activities after taxation		(1.2)	3.6
Attributable to minority interests		(2.2)	(2.3)
(Loss) profit for the year	17	(3.4)	1.3

Figure 2.1   Rugby Football Union Profit and Loss Account

Source: From the Rugby Football Union Annual Report 2006.

Can you see how the statements use similar terminology and layout? Granted some of the finer details are slightly different but in general they are the same. This similarity is also highlighted in the balance sheet (see Figure 2.2).

Again many of the terms and structure are identical. If you think about why this is, and approach the question logically, you will be able to understand both the need for a regulatory framework and why this chapter is here. Just consider that you are preparing a list of the top performances by 100 metre sprinters. When you look at the times that the individual sprinters have recorded you will take it for granted that they all comply with

Balance sheets

at 30 June 2006

	Notes	Group 2006 £m	Group 2005 restated £m	Parent 2006 £m	Parent 2005 restated £m
Fixed assets					
Tangible fixed assets	6	**100.9**	63.4	**99.4**	62.1
Loans	7	**4.4**	2.6	**0.4**	0.5
Investments	8	**(0.3)**	(0.2)	**25.2**	25.2
		105.0	65.8	**125.0**	87.8
Current assets					
Stocks		**0.9**	1.3	**0.7**	1.2
Debtors and prepayments	9	**16.2**	17.5	**27.4**	17.6
Cash at bank and in hand		**28.0**	43.8	**18.5**	39.4
		45.1	62.6	**46.6**	58.2
Creditors:					
Amounts falling due within one year	10	**(22.6)**	(17.3)	**(22.7)**	(14.6)
Net current assets		**22.5**	45.3	**23.9**	43.6
Total assets less current liabilities		**127.5**	111.1	**148.9**	131.4
Creditors:					
Amounts falling due after one year	11	**(1.2)**	(0.6)	**(1.2)**	(0.6)
Provisions for liabilities and charges	13	**(3.5)**	(5.0)	**(3.4)**	(4.9)
		122.8	105.5	**144.3**	125.9
Pension liability		**(0.8)**	(1.2)	**(0.8)**	(1.2)
		122.0	104.3	**143.5**	124.7
Financed by:					
Debentures 2075–2081	14	**78.8**	57.4	**78.8**	57.4
Capital and reserves					
Called up share capital	15	**–**	–	**–**	–
Debenture premium account	16	**38.1**	38.1	**38.1**	38.1
Profit and loss account	17	**4.0**	7.0	**26.6**	29.2
Total shareholders' funds		**42.1**	45.1	**64.7**	67.3
Minority interests		**1.1**	1.8	**–**	–
Capital employed		**122.0**	104.3	**143.5**	124.7

Figure 2.2 Rugby Football Union Balance Sheet

Source: From the Rugby Football Union Annual Report 2006.

certain rules and regulations (e.g. run on a flat track, not wind assisted etc.). Similarly, when looking at the performance of businesses, you need to be able to make similar assumptions with a view to making comparisons either from year to year for the same company or to benchmark against other companies. Just as with any type of information, accounts need to be objective, reliable, comparable and understandable.

Small businesses and local swimming clubs, for example, can prepare their accounts in any style they like. However, it is generally accepted that their accounts will follow certain principles that form an accepted code of practice for accountants so that they match the requirements of 'good information'. However, companies must comply with the requirements of the Companies Act 1985 (CA 1985), and, as amended, by the Companies Act 1989. A major requirement of this act was that each year companies must prepare financial statements that give 'a true and fair view'. This is so that their shareholders can see how the company is performing. A copy of these statements will be submitted to Companies House so that if a member of the public wishes to see what is going on they can get access to the information. Generally these statements will be in the form of an annual report, which we will look at in more detail later. Company law is just one source of the rules and guidelines that seek to regulate how company accounts are prepared. The other sources will now be introduced.

THE REGULATORY FRAMEWORK

The regulations over UK company accounts are framed by several sources:

Company Law

The major requirements of the CA 1985 were outlined above. The act also recognised 'statements of standard accounting practice' (SSAPs). These were the predecessors of the Financial Reporting Standards (FRSs). Perhaps the most important SSAP was SSAP 2, which covered the 'Disclosure of accounting policies', and dealt with the fundamental concepts of accounting. This has now been 'updated' by FRS 18 which we will look at a little later. The reason for stating this is not to bore you with detail but so that if you happen to hear such phrases as 'In order to comply with SSAP X or FRS Y' you will have an idea of what is meant. Figure 2.3 illustrates the type of claims that the RFU makes in its financial statements so that whoever reads them knows what is going on.

---

1. Accounting policies
The financial statements have been prepared under the historical cost convention and in accordance with applicable UK accounting standards. A summary of the significant group accounting policies is set out below, together with an explanation of where charges have been made to previous policies on the adoption of new accounting standards in the year.

(a) Changes in accounting policies
The group has adopted FRS17 'Retirement benefits' and FRS28 'Corresponding amounts' in these financial statements. The adoption of these standards represents a change in accounting policy and the comparative figures have been restated accordingly except where the exemption to restate comparative has been taken. Details of the effect of the prior year adjustments are given in note 17.

Figure 2.3 Rugby Football Union Statement of accounting policies

Source: From the Rugby Football Union Annual Report 2006.

Financial Reporting Standards

The increasing complexities of the business world (including sport!) meant that there was a requirement to develop accounting standards to prevent the misrepresentation of profits and to narrow the areas of difference and variety of accounting practice. Therefore a body entitled the Accounting Standards Committee (ASC) was set up with the objective of reducing the 'flexibility' that allowed companies to be somewhat 'creative' with financial information. The ASC issued accounting standards, known as Statements of Standard Accounting Practice (SSAPs). Unfortunately the ASC did not have the power to improve the quality of financial reporting, so, in 1990, the Financial Reporting Council (FRC) was established to deal with corporate reporting and governance. However, the ASC was soon replaced by the Accounting Standards Board (ASB), which began to issue accounting standards known as Financial Reporting Standards (FRSs). The aims of the ASB are 'to establish and improve standards of financial accounting and reporting for the benefit of users, preparers and auditors of financial information'.

International Accounting Standards

The International Accounting Standards Committee (IASC) was established in June 1973 with an overriding aim to co-ordinate the development of International Accounting Standards. If you think for a minute you'll realise that the international dimension to accounting is of vital importance to sport given that many areas of the industry are not confined to business in the UK. Globalisation, sponsorship and broadcasting have given sport in the UK a platform to establish a worldwide audience. The IASC includes representatives from many different countries from across the globe as well as from the UK. Since its establishment it has however been superseded by the International Accounting Standards Board (IASB) which itself issues International Financial Reporting Standards (IFRSs). Since January 2005, companies are required to publish their financial statements using IFRSs rather than domestic standards.

The stock exchange

The stock exchange is a place or 'market' where stocks and shares (i.e. a share of the ownership of companies) are bought and sold. When companies trade their shares this way, they are known as a 'listed' or 'quoted' company. Some UK-based sport organisations are listed themselves, for example Arena Leisure (which you looked at in Chapter 1), the Blacks Leisure Group (which sells outdoor clothing and equipment), Dominos Pizza, Ladbrokes and Southampton Leisure Holdings (Southampton Football Club to us). Being listed will allow companies to grow by raising more capital by issuing more shares. It also allows people to buy shares in the company, and obviously allows existing shareholders to sell their holdings. Consequently the ownership, and control, of companies can be bought here. If you are a football fan you may remember what happened to Manchester United plc in the summer of 2004 when the American tycoon Malcolm Glazer first bought a number of shares in the business and then eventually de-listed the company after having purchased all of the shares.

In order for a company to be 'listed' it must conform to the rules and regulations stated by the Stock Exchange. The company will commit itself to certain procedures and standards including how information is disclosed. This includes publishing an annual report within six months of the year-end and publishing interim results giving profit and loss information.

ACTIVITY

Go to the financial times website (www.ft.com/) and have a look the 'Annual Reports Service' link and select 'Leisure and Entertainment'. Here you will find a selection of different Sport and Leisure companies listed. Once you have done so try and answer the following questions.

1   How many sport organisations are listed?
2   How many leisure organisations are listed?
3   Which sector, sport or leisure, is represented the most on the UK Stock Exchange?
4   Is your favourite sport team listed?

In total there are about 30 listed organisations on the 'free' site. However, do not be fooled, as this is just a small proportion of the actual number. Of these 30 there is only one notable sport organisation – Southampton Leisure Holdings plc, however you may also have noticed Powerleague Group plc as we mentioned these earlier in the book. What this exercise should have shown is that 'Leisure' organisations are more likely to list themselves on the stock exchange due to the size of the market that they operate within. Furthermore, when sport organisations float on the exchange it can bring about significant problems.

FOOTBALL, THE STOCK EXCHANGE AND MANCHESTER UNITED FOOTBALL CLUB

Malcolm Glazer, the US sports tycoon and owner of the Tampa Bay Buccaneers (an American Football Team), won full control of Manchester United plc in a £790m takeover in June 2005. The takeover was not without controversy as many of the club's fans tried desperately to stop it from happening. However, the opportunity for Glazer came because Manchester United plc was a listed company. Let's have a quick look at why this came about and what the implications could be.

After Manchester United was floated on the UK stock exchange in 1990 and following a surge of investment in shares (i.e. small bits of the business that you and I could buy) the club went from strength to strength. Its biggest achievement to date was the 1999 treble winning season when it was victorious in the English Premier League, the FA Cup and the UEFA Champions' League. Such success had turned Manchester United into one of the biggest global brands in sport and made it an unlikely takeover candidate – after all the company was estimated to be worth somewhere in the region of £670m. Rupert Murdoch and BskyB had attempted it in the past but the Office of Fair Trading prevented that particular move.

The main problem for anyone attempting a takeover is to get into a position whereby they can acquire 75 per cent of the shares. At this point the company can be de-listed – preventing you and me from buying any shares – and at 90 per cent a compulsory purchase of the remaining 10 per cent of shares can be made. Nevertheless, Glazer managed not only to gain control of the club through his takeover vehicle Red Football, but also to convert it into a completely private company.

Although it took a while, the mechanics of the takeover were simple. While keeping his holding ticking over Glazer knew that he would have to convince the major shareholders to part with their investments. Shares are generally purchased by financial gain, i.e. you buy them to make money. At the beginning of May 2005 a Manchester United Football Club (MUFC) share was worth around £2.60 so to get the major shareholders to sell he would have to offer more. Glazer effectively mounted his takeover bid by securing the 28.7 per cent stake owned by Irish racing tycoons J. P. McManus and John Magnier. The racing duo agreed to sell all of their shares for £3.00 each and in doing so made a sizeable profit on their invest-ment. This purchase was in addition to the shares that he had already purchased by offering shareholders around 20 per cent more than the company was worth.

Hence the stock market value was about £670m, a clear £120m less than he eventually paid. The timeline of how this came about is shown in Table 2.1.

Table 2.1 Manchester United Football Club takeover timeline

March 2003	Malcolm Glazer makes his first move and purchases a 2.9% stake in the club.
June 2004	After 12 months of activity Glazer's stake in MUFC nears 20%.
October 2004	The MUFC Board receives a bid approach from Glazer as his holding approaches 30%.
February 2005	A new approach is made by Glazer valuing the club at £800m.
12th May 2005	Glazer raises his stake to 57 per cent and launches a formal takeover bid.
23rd May 2005	Having purchased the stakes of major shareholders McManus and Magnier (28.7 per cent), Glazer now owns more than 76 per cent of the club.
28th June 2005	Glazer secures 98 per cent and therefore total control of the club.

Although Glazer was eventually successful with his takeover of the club, in doing so he has had to borrow heavily against the club's assets and take out a number of potentially high-risk loans alongside his own personal investment. MUFC was a financially stable business that regularly made a profit and had plenty of readily available cash to fund the acquisition of new players and ground expansions. Some will argue that that position is relatively precarious. Glazer has gambled that future on-the-field success will bring about increased revenues which will enable him to repay the debts quickly. It could be viewed as a good move. As was mentioned earlier MUFC is a global brand and a very successful club. If MUFC is to continue its growth as one of the biggest club teams in the world it will need to maintain its position as a global force. It is documented that this will be achieved by exploiting markets such as TV revenue to a greater extent, increasing ticket prices and arranging lucrative tours to the Far East and the USA. Only time will tell if Glazer gets it right.

Shares in Manchester United were de-listed after 14 years of trading and examining how this came about provides a useful insight into how sound financial ideas can have a varied effect. By floating the club on the stock exchange the MUFC board was able to raise the necessary funds to mount a serious challenge to the top teams in England and Europe. To an extent the decision was vindicated when you consider the list of honours that the club has won over the time since floatation. Briefly these are; eight EPL titles, four FA Cups, one League Cup, one European Cup Winners Cup, one UCL title and one Intercontinental Cup. As mentioned, they were an unlikely takeover target due to the value of the business. However, when you list a business on the stock market anyone with a big enough pocket can launch a takeover bid.

FRS 18 accounting policies

We will look at FRS 18 because it gives an insight into the rules, concepts and conventions used by accountants. FRS 18 deals with the selection, application and disclosure of accounting policies. Its objective is to ensure that for all material items:

- An entity adopts the accounting policies most appropriate to its particular circumstances for the purpose of giving a true and fair view;
- The accounting policies adopted are reviewed regularly to ensure that they remain appropriate, and are changed when a new policy becomes more appropriate to the entity's particular circumstances; and
- Sufficient information is disclosed in the financial statements to enable users to understand the accounting policies adopted and how they have been implemented.

FRS 18 states that an entity should judge the appropriateness of accounting policies to its particular circumstances against the objectives of relevance, reliability, comparability and understandability.

Relevance

Financial information is relevant if it has the ability to influence the economic decisions of users and is provided in time to influence those decisions.

Reliability

Financial information is reliable if:

- it reflects the substance of the transactions and other events that have taken place;
- it is free from deliberate or systematic bias (i.e. it is 'neutral');
- it is free from material error;
- it is complete within the bounds of materiality;
- under conditions of uncertainty, it has been prudently prepared (i.e. a degree of caution has been exercised).

The rationale for being 'prudent' is to guard the business against the over-estimation of income and under-estimation of expenses in financial statements. Although revenues and profits should not be anticipated, losses should be accounted for as soon as they arise or are likely to arise. A good example of the prudence concept will arise when we look at stock (inventory) transactions. A retailer will buy goods to sell at higher price and thereby make a profit. So how much is the stock worth? It could be argued that its value to the retailer is what it will be sold for, but that assumes that it will be sold. What if there is a change of fashion? What if there is a surplus of that type of good and the stock has to be discounted to move it on? Both of these will change the future worth of the stock and consequently to avoid such future disappointments the stock will be valued at the cost price in the balance sheet (or if lower, the future expected selling price).

Comparability

Information increases in value to its users if it can be compared with similar information about the company or with that of other companies. Such comparability can be achieved through a combination of consistency and disclosure.

Consistency means that:

1 Similar items within a single set of accounts should be given similar accounting treatment (for example the percentage depreciation written off from fixed asset values).
2 The same treatment should be applied from one accounting period to the next for similar items so that one year's results are comparable to the next.

Two concepts are highlighted in FRS 18 as playing a key role in financial statements and hence in the selection of accounting policies. These two concepts are 'going concern' and 'accruals'.

Going concern

The information presented in the financial statements is prepared on the basis that the organisation will continue to operate for the foreseeable future. This is because users of the statements will normally want to assess the potential for the entity to generate future cash flows and will not be interested in the break up value of the assets.

Accruals

The accruals basis of accounting requires the non-cash effects of transactions and other events to be reflected in the financial statements for the accounting period in which they occur and not in the period when the cash is paid or received. For example, if a sale is agreed in 2006 but the terms of the deal are that the cash is not received until 2007, the transaction should be shown in the accounts for 2006.

Other concepts

Some other terms and concepts that underpin the thinking and actions of accountants and the accounts that they produce are:

- *Materiality*: this means that only items of significance are included in the financial statements. An item is significant if its omission or misrepresentation could influence the economic decisions of those using the financial statements; for example the British Triathlon Association would record that it owns some racing bikes but it would not record that it had 50 paper bib numbers left over from an event that they staged.
- The *business entity concept* dictates that a line is drawn between the business and its owner(s): the business and its owner(s) are two separate entities. The financial statements will therefore be drawn up from the perspective of the business and not its owner(s). You saw how this works in practice when we covered legal identity.
- The *money measurement concept* simply means that only items of monetary value can be recorded in a set of financial statements; for example the stock that Blacks Leisure group has to sell in its stores will be shown but the business skills of its store managers will not. The financial statements of an organisation will show the success of the management team but the skills and intellect cannot be given a monetary value and placed in the statements.
- The *dual aspect concept* recognises that each transaction conducted by a business will affect two items within the business. For example if the business buys stock then it will have an increase in the value of stock. If cash is used to buy the stock then the amount of cash available will decrease. We will examine this particular concept in much more detail later.
- The *historical cost concept* dictates that the value of items that a business owns must be based on their original cost and must not be adjusted for any subsequent changes in price or value. Much debate surrounds this concept because certain items such as land and buildings will probably change significantly in value over time and using the historical cost is not necessarily the most accurate way of estimating value. None the less, this is what accounts have to do!

The RFU has to ensure that it conforms to all of the concepts and policies that relate to its business and disclose in its annual report exactly how it has constructed its financial statements. Have a look at Figure 2.4 to see what we mean.

Statement of the Management Board's responsibilities in respect of the financial statements

The Friendly and Industrial and Provident Societies Act 1968 requires the Management Board to prepare financial statements for each financial year which give a true and fair view of the affairs of the Rugby Football Union and of its income and expenditure for that period. In preparing these financial statements, the Management Board is required to:

- select suitable accounting policies and apply them consistently;

- make the necessary judgements and estimates which are both reasonable and prudent; and

- prepare the financial statements on a going concern basis, unless it is inappropriate to presume that the Rugby Football Union will continue in business.

The Management Board is responsible for keeping proper books of account with respect to the transactions and assets and liabilities of the Union. Such books must enable a true and fair view to be given of its affairs and explain its transactions. The Management Board has a general responsibility for taking such steps as are reasonably open to it to safeguard the assets of the Union and to prevent fraud and other irregularities.

Figure 2.4 Rugby Football Union Statement of Responsibility

Source: From the Rugby Football Union Annual Report 2006.

Note: The regulatory framework has changed over the years and will continue to change as new ideas and opinions are discussed. However, the bottom line, for you, is that if you grasp the concepts, principles and guidelines discussed above, which are the building blocks of accountancy, you will be able develop with them. We will regularly see the effects of these concepts throughout the remainder of this book and consequently your knowledge and appreciation of them will grow.

MORE ACCOUNTING TERMINOLOGY

You may have come across one or two terms now that you may not be fully comfortable with so before we move on it is worth reinforcing some of the more regularly used terms so that you can begin to use them when communicating accounting information – we touched on some of these in Chapter 1.

ASSETS

These are items or resources that have a value to the business and things that are used by the business and for the business. Normally we will classify assets as either fixed or current. The basic difference being that a fixed asset is something that the business intends to keep and use for some time whereas a current asset is held for the business to convert into cash during trading. Some good examples here are business premises, motor vehicles that are fixed assets and stock and cash, which are current assets.

INTANGIBLE FIXED ASSET

These are things that have a value but are not tangible. For example a royalty – it has a value (people have to pay you) but it is not a physical item – goodwill, patents and tradeworks.

TANGIBLE FIXED ASSETS

These are tangible, i.e. they are physical items, for example property, equipment, machines, vehicles, furniture.

LIABILITIES

Amounts owed by the business to people other than the owner. Normally we will see liabilities classified as either payable within one year e.g. bank overdrafts, supplier accounts, or payable after one year e.g. longer-term bank loans.

CAPITAL

This is generally considered to be the owners' stake in the business and may also be called equity. To take this a step further it is also the excess of assets over liabilities.

DEBTOR

An entity or person who owes money to the business.

CREDITOR

An entity or person to whom money is owed.

DEPRECIATION

This a notional charge made in the accounts to represent the use of an asset. It also serves to reduce the value of an asset in the balance sheet.

THE IMPACT OF THE REGULATORY FRAMEWORK ON SPORT

By now you are probably wondering why you need to know all of this to understand accounts. The answer is simple. In 1997 the ASB issued its tenth financial reporting standard, or FRS 10. This has since become one of the single most important changes to the world of sport business, and in particular professional team sport, as it reclassified the way in which professional clubs could value their players and record them onto the balance sheet. In a nutshell, the balance sheet has a section at the top where businesses classify 'Goodwill and Intangible Assets'. Although the terminology will be meaningless to you at this stage what we need you to understand is that there needs to be a way of valuing every item on the balance sheet. This is mainly because it has long been argued that some of the more traditional financial reporting policies didn't allow for a full understanding and consideration of issues relating to professional sports clubs and in particular football clubs. One of the main issues was that clubs operated different systems for the treatment of items such as transfer fees, grants and sponsorship.

FRS 10 and professional team sport

Accounting problems are well documented in the world of professional team sport and although some of the practices are improving through the involvement of professional advisors, greater financial awareness and increased media interest, some questions still remain. Think for a minute about how a professional sports club should revalue their property assets, for example stadiums, after they have been redeveloped. How do they reduce (depreciate) the value of these assets and, given the loyalty of fans and the power of brand names on a global platform how can clubs recognise their brand names as accounting assets? However, the most prominent question for clubs in any sport is how to best record the investment made in players?

The introduction of FRS 10 means that there is now consistency in the area of 'Goodwill and Intangible Assets', which begins to address the questions outlined above. Under the rule, when a club purchases a player through the transfer market it has to include the cost of acquiring the player's registration as an intangible fixed asset (Define ITA) on the balance sheet. Each year thereafter, the registration cost has to be written off as an expense (amortised) through the profit and loss account until the player's contract expires. Look at Figure 2.5 and see how Southampton Football Club demonstrates that it does this.

INTANGIBLE FIXED ASSETS

The element of each player's transfer fee which relates to his registration is capitalised as an intangible asset and amortised over the period of his contract including any agreed extensions, subject to any provision for impairment. Contingent fees payable, which are dependent upon the number of first team appearances and international debuts made, are capitalised in the period when it is considered probable that the conditions of the contract will be satisfied.

The profit or loss arising out of the disposal of players' registrations represent the difference between the consideration receiveable, net of any transaction costs, and the unamortised cost of the intangible asset.

TANGIBLE FIXED ASSETS

Tangible fixed assets are stated at cost net of depreciation and any provision for impairment.

Figure 2.5 Southampton Football Club Asset Statement

Source: From Southampton Leisure Holdings Plc Annual Report and Accounts 2006.

Before the rule was introduced there was no way of valuing players on a balance sheet despite the fact that they were important assets. Because of this some clubs began to develop ways of including the costs and purchases of players. However, this was done internally and without direction from the Accounting Standards Board. Consequently the introduction of FRS 10 gives the consistency required for us to confidently compare the financial results of professional sports teams. Such analysis will be examined later in this book. The notes in Figure 2.6 illustrate how Southampton Football club addresses FRS 10.

Again these excerpts are here to show you that the regulatory framework and statement of accounting policies and concepts must be used at all times when the financial statements are constructed. Don't worry about any unfamiliar terminology, as we will cover it later.

CORPORATE GOVERNANCE

Organisations, and their accountants, should behave like good citizens. Laws, ethics and social responsibility should influence their behaviour. However, not all citizens are good. Similarly neither are all organisations, directors, accountants and auditors! Consequently scandals such as Enron and WorldCom and some high profile companies going bankrupt led to accountants facing the scrutiny and mistrust that is usually reserved for politicians and wayward sports stars!

NOTES TO THE ACCOUNTS CONTINUED
PERIOD ENDED 30 JUNE 2006

11. INTANGIBLE FIXED ASSETS

Group	Goodwill £'000	Player registration £'000	Total £'000
COST			
At 1 June 2005	1,026	35,393	36,419
Additions	–	2,688	2,688
Disposals	–	(23,975)	(23,975)
AT 30 JUNE 2006	**1,026**	**14,106**	**15,132**
ACCUMULATED AMORTISATION			
At 1 June 2005	128	23,036	23,164
Charge for the period	111	4,574	4,685
Impairment losses	–	734	734
Disposals	–	(17,208)	(17,208)
AT 30 JUNE 2006	**239**	**11,136**	**11,375**
NET BOOK VALUE			
AT 30 JUNE 2006	**787**	**2,970**	**3,757**
At 31 May 2005	898	12,357	13,255

Amortisation of player registrations is normally calculated on a straight-line basis. Where appropriate, adjustments are made to reflect the specific circumstances of individual players. The accounts include additional charges on this basis of £734,000 (2005: £732,000).

Figure 2.6 Southampton Football Club Asset Figures

Source: From Southampton Leisure Holdings Plc Annual Report and Accounts 2006.

Accounting bodies, accountants, institutional investors, audit firms etc. responded by promoting 'corporate governance'. The Organisation for Economic Co-operation and Development (OECD) defines corporate governance by stating that the systems by which organisations are directed and controlled involve 'a set of relationships between a company's management, its board, its shareholders and other stakeholders [that provides] a structure through which the objectives of the company are set and the means of attaining those objectives and monitoring performance are determined'.

The major guide to corporate governance in the UK is the '2003 Combined Code'. The code gives guidance of 'best practice' in four categories:

- Boards of directors
- Executive remuneration
- Financial reporting and internal control
- Shareholder relations.

the 'rules' of financial accounting

The Combined Code is *not* a legal requirement: it lays out 'principles'. However the Stock Exchange requires that all listed companies *must* include in their financial statements:

- a statement of how they applied the principles of the Combined Code;
- explanations, which give reasons if they did not comply with any of the provisions, set out in the Combined Code.

Although corporate governance is generally thought of as being aimed at listed companies the principles should apply to any organisation. Governance is a global issue and many countries have developed their own ideas on corporate governance. In America the system is 'rules based'. The rules are stated in the Sarbanes Oxley Act (2002). Companies and audit firms must comply with the Act if they want to avoid 20 years in prison and huge fines!

Perhaps the best way for you to remember and understand the scope of governance is 'F –TRIADS'. This acronym is based on the seven characteristics of good governance as identified in the King Report from South Africa:

F: fairness

T: transparency

R: responsibility

I: independence

A: accountability

D: discipline

S: social responsibility

Sport and Leisure organisations much like any normal business will have their own governance frameworks. These should conform to the F-TRIADS acronym. The threat of litigation almost forces the organisations that we are concerned with to disclose how they consider corporate governance on an annual basis. Normally statements will be made about how the principles are covered in an organisation's annual report (such as the excerpt shown in Figure 2.7. Be aware that this is only a selection of what has been written by the RFU on the matter). You should, however, note that providing that you are fair, transparent, responsible, independent, accountable, disciplined and show a degree of common sense when working with financial information you will be fine.

Corporate Governance

One of the objectives in the Union's Strategic Plan is that the RFU will be managed to Plc standards, particularly regarding effective management and corporate governance. The Management Board acknowledges the value of the principles of good governance as set out in the Combined Code, both in terms of ensuring integrity and accountability in the management of the Union's affairs, and also in increasing the effectiveness and efficiency of the Union's business. To that end the union has adopted certain principles associated with best practice in corporate governance. The following statements describe how these principles have been applied in the period under review.

Management Board

The Management Board's powers are clearly defined in the Rules of the Rugby Football Union, particularly Rule 12. It has clear terms of reference and standing orders and consists of three executive directors, together with ten other members representing a broad cross section of the game of rugby who do not have executive responsibilities. There is a clear division of responsibility between the roles of the non-executive Chairman and the Chief Executive, and all executive directors have agreed job descriptions and limits of authority. The Board meets at least ten times each year and considers matters under its terms of reference, which include the development of the Union's strategic plan, allocation of financial resources, reviewing the performance of executive directors, approval of annual budgets, considering the recommendation of the Board's Standing Committees, whose responsibilities relate to policy development, and monitoring of the performance of the Union's subsidiary and associated companies.

Figure 2.7 Rugby Football Union Corporate Governance

Source: From the Rugby Football Union Annual Report 2006.

Do you feel confident or confused at this point? Although there are a wide variety of accounting concepts, rules and regulations you only have to be aware of them, unlike the poor accountants who have to use them each and every day. The International and UK accounting standards bodies provide order for you, which will ultimately make your life much easier when we come to dissect accounts, and begin to understand what they really mean.

By the end of this book you will understand all of the concepts that the examples use and in most cases be able to make any adjustments to the financial statements. At this point all you need is a general awareness of the key issues raised in this chapter. To see if you have grasped a general understanding try the review questions below.

QUESTIONS FOR REVIEW

1   List the accounting concepts and principles that you can remember from this chapter.
2   For the following statements fill in the blanks.

a   The _____ concept recognises that each transaction conducted by a business will affect two items within the business.

b   The _____ concept dictates that information presented in the financial statements is prepared on the basis that the organisation will continue to operate for the foreseeable future.

c   Only items of significance are included in the financial statements because accountants apply the _____ concept.

d   The _____ concept dictates that a line is drawn between the business and its owner(s): the business and its owner(s) are two separate entities.

e   The _____ basis of accounting requires the non-cash effects of transactions and other events to be reflected in the financial statements for the accounting period in which they occur and not in the period when the cash is paid or received.

f   The _____ concept simply means that only items of monetary value can be recorded in a set of financial statements.

3   Identify three of the regulatory bodies that oversee accounting.

4   Are these statements true or false?

    a Assets are items or resources that have a value to the business and things that are used by the business and for the business.

    b Liabilities are amounts owed to the business by other people.

    c Capital is generally considered to be the owners' stake in the business and may also be called equity.

    d Debtors are an entity or person who owes money to the business.

    e Creditors are amounts owned by the business that are of value.

the 'rules' of financial accounting

1 Hopefully you remembered some of the following accounting concepts:

- Reliability
- Comparability
- Going concern
- Accruals
- Materiality
- Business entity
- Money measurement
- Dual aspect
- Historical cost

2 The blanks should have been filled in as follows;

a Dual aspect
b Going concern
c Materiality
d Business entity
e Accruals
f Money measurement

3 Financial Reporting Council, International Accounting Standards Committee and the stock exchange.

4 True or false answers below:

a True
b False: Liabilities are amounts owed by the business to other people
c True
d True
e False: Creditors are liabilities and are therefore amounts owed by the business

PART 2
THE MECHANICS

CHAPTER THREE

FINANCIAL ACCOUNTING – THE MECHANICS

On completion of this chapter you will be able to:

- Understand and communicate the process of the accounting system.
- Understand the accounting equation and its impact on financial statements.
- Understand and use the principles of double-entry bookkeeping.

INTRODUCTION

You already know that every type of sports organisation, large or small, will produce a set of financial statements. In Chapter 1 we told you that our aim was not to teach you how to be accountants so you've probably got another question for us – why have we have included a section on the mechanics of financial accounting? The answer to this is twofold. First, it's because many of you will have to use financial information and when doing so you may need to trace where certain facts and figures have come from. Second, it is because many of you studying courses related to Sport Management and Sport and Leisure Management will be expected to have an understanding of how financial transactions are recorded. Looking beyond academic expectations, we think that it is a useful skill to have and one that will increase your employability. Just imagine how impressive it will be when you have a job interview and can demonstrate that you have a sound understanding of financial accounting. The information included in this chapter and Chapters 4, 5 and 6 will help you to understand the technical issues that are fundamental in the learning process that will facilitate your understanding of financial statements.

Organisations need to record economic transactions so that they can produce financial statements (such as those illustrated in Chapters 1 and 2) and to do this they require an accounting system. A series of procedures will be established so that the organisation records every transaction that happens. For each transaction the amount, the date and a description will be required so that those responsible for the organisation are aware of what has happened, when it happened and the financial consequences.

43

The basic accounting system is commonly known as double-entry bookkeeping and although most organisations now use computerised programmes these derive their 'logic' from the basic system. Consequently it will be good for you to understand the logic that drives such systems. The specific application and style of the accounting system will depend on the type and size of business. Most large organisations will have accountants on their staff but small businesses and organisations are more likely to hire 'external' accountants. It is therefore unlikely that you will have to perform specific accounting duties as part of your future role but it is a certainty that if you are a manager you will have to talk to the accountants (and on a regular basis!).

As a result we only really need to focus on the things that you may have to do in smaller businesses such as sole traders or partnerships, although the general principles that we use apply to *all* organisations. For this reason the examples used in this chapter will be based on a company called Kitlocker, a team and leisure wear provider. This organisation will be used throughout the next few chapters as it provides us with a real life example to illustrate the basic points. We could use a professional sports club or team or even a large leisure organisation. The problem, however, with doing it with one of those examples is the level of detail that is required. You do not need that level of depth and besides it gets rather confusing! If you want to know a little more about Kitlocker you can go online and have a look (www.kitlocker.com).

CASE STUDY

KITLOCKER: AN INTRODUCTION

Business partners Mike Kent and Tom Ward established Kitlocker in May 2005. The principal aim of the business is to provide team kit, leisure wear and branding solutions to university sport teams. However, following a successful launch the company has set up a website to cater for a much wider market including colleges, schools and the general public.

A bit of history

The idea of Kitlocker came from Mike and Tom's involvement with club and university volleyball. Having both played the sport for a number of years they noticed that the suppliers of team volleyball kit (including leisure wear) were not meeting the requirements of their customers. The lead-time on deliveries and general variety of goods available were not up to standard. After talking to friends who played other sports they soon realised that there was a clear gap in the market to provide kit that was fit for purpose, easily obtainable and at realistic 'student' prices.

Moreover, while involved on a Sport Management degree programme Mike was given an assignment brief to come up with a business idea and produce a business

44

plan. Having noticed the potential for success in the university sport kit market Mike decided to set up, on paper, Kitlocker. The market research that he conducted supported what he and Tom had discovered while playing volleyball on the British Universities Sports Association (BUSA) circuit. This was enough for them to consider setting up the business for real so they took their plan to a professional enterprise agency for consideration.

The result

The feedback from the enterprise agency was positive and with relatively low start up costs Mike and Tom made the decision to go live with the project once Mike had completed his studies. Consequently, Kitlocker was formally established as a business partnership on 28 May 2005. In the beginning they had some important decisions to make: how to source goods, how to sell goods and how to get their company known by their market.

The marketing and sales solution was simple and they set up a website (www.Kitlocker.com) which was used as their interface with their customers. At first this was fairly straightforward with basic listings by sport. A customer would log on to the site and order what they wanted. However, this did not serve the university teams well as it relied on team secretaries collating orders, collecting money and arranging delivery. As a result in 2006 they launched a new version of the website which is now linked to individual universities. Customers go to their university link, select their sport and then order bespoke kit related to the team.

The finance

At start up Mike and Tom invested around £6,000 of personal capital, which was supplemented by a start-up grant for small businesses of £3,500. This gave them the necessary funds to purchase a laser cutting machine to help them design bespoke logos for sport teams and to have a professionally designed e-commerce website created. In addition to this they arranged a leasing agreement for two heat-sealing machines that allowed them to put their designs onto actual kit.

SUMMARY

This provides you with a brief overview of Kitlocker, which we will come back to regularly during this chapter and again throughout the book. The Kitlocker partnership will be used to illustrate a number of key financial decisions and help you to put the theory you are learning into practice.

RECORDING BUSINESS TRANSACTIONS

In Chapter 2 we briefly mentioned the 'Dual Aspect Concept': this means that every transaction will affect two 'items' within the business. The effect on both items must be recognised so that the transaction is recorded correctly. Every transaction will have either an increasing (+) or a decreasing (–) effect on an item (or account). An increase in one account will mean that another account will decrease but given that some accounts are for assets and others are for liabilities they both might increase and decrease. Confused? Good! At least it shows that you are thinking! We will solve this riddle and many more during this chapter.

However, before we go any further you need to remember that the business entity concept states that business transactions are recorded from the point of view of the business (not the owner). In other words the business and its owners are two separate legal identities and as such must be viewed from an accounting perspective as being totally separate bodies. However they can, and do, carry out transactions with each other. For example, as soon as a business starts up it will need some cash. The owner will lend cash to the business. The business will now have an asset: cash. By the dual aspect concept, something else must happen too. The business will now have a liability: it owes money to the owner. This debt to the owner by the business is part of the 'capital structure' of the business, i.e. how it is financed. The organisation may also be financed (get its cash or acquire assets) by other sources such as a loan from a bank or by taking credit from suppliers. Remember how Kitlocker was financed? The company was set up with £9,500 in cash, which was made up of £6,000 of personal funds and a grant of £3,500. A rough balance sheet for the organisation would therefore look something like what is shown in Table 3.1.

Table 3.1 Kitlocker and its start-up Balance Sheet

	£	£
Assets		
Non-current assets		
Property, plant and equipment		0
Current Assets		
Inventories		
Cash and cash equivalents	9500	
		9500
Total assets		9500
Equity and Liabilities		
Equity		9500
Non-current liabilities		
Current Liabilities		
Trade and other payables		0
Total equity and liabilities		9500

THE ACCOUNTING EQUATION

The relationship between all of the assets, liabilities and capital of an organisation forms what accountants call the 'Accounting Equation'. This simple relationship governs the recording and presentation of all financial transactions. It must always balance! The equation is:

Assets = Capital + Liabilities

or if we move it around

Assets – Liabilities = Capital)

This shows that the assets of the organisation must equal the total of the combined value of capital and other liabilities, that is to say the equation must balance! The equation could be Assets = Liabilities, as 'capital' is a liability but it is always better to identify capital separately ('capital' is the amount of resources provided by the owners of the business). Let's have another look at Kitlocker and see how some of its early business decisions affected its accounting equation.

KITLOCKER AND THE ACCOUNTING EQUATION

To begin with Kitlocker had £9,500 so its accounting equation would have looked something like this

Assets = Capital + Liabilities

£9,500 (Asset, Cash) = £9,500 (Capital) + £0 (Liabilities)

Fairly easy? We hope so because now we are going to show you how the equation changes when business decisions are made and how you can rearrange the equation should you wish to do so. Think back to the first part of this case study where you saw what Kitlocker did with their start-up capital. The first thing they did was to purchase a laser cutting machine which cost the company £1,800. Do you think that their accounting equation changed to reflect the transaction?

Hopefully you said 'no'. Although they have purchased something it is classified as an asset. The company used the asset of cash to get the asset of machinery. If we get technical here they have traded a current asset for a fixed asset. Have a look at how the accounting equation is now.

£9,500 (Assets) = £9,500 (Capital) + £0

or

£1,800 (Fixed Asset, Machine) + £7,700 (Current Asset, Cash) = £9,500 (Capital) + £0 (Liabilities)

47

Once in existence the company began making sales. In doing so it needed to buy things from suppliers and sell them to customers. One of its transactions was to purchase 20 hooded sweatshirts from a local supplier. These hoodies cost the company £200 which it paid immediately. What will the accounting equation look like now? Hopefully something like this.

$$£1,800 \text{ (FA, Machine)} + £7,500 \text{ (CA, Cash)} + £200 \text{ (CA, Stock)} = £9,500$$
$$\text{(Capital)} + £0 \text{ (Liabilities)}$$

This is all very well but also very easy. Consider now that Kitlocker purchases 100 rugby jerseys from an Italian supplier for £1,500. Instead of paying for them immediately they put them on credit, i.e. they agree to pay for them at a later date (usually 28 days after the invoice date). What will this do to the accounting equation?

$$£1,800 \text{ (FA, Machine)} + £7,500 \text{ (CA, Cash)} + £1,700 \text{ (CA, Stock)} = £9,500$$
$$\text{(Capital)} + £1,500 \text{ (Liabilities, Creditors)}$$

Hopefully you got this but if you didn't it may well be because you've forgotten some of the terminology that you looked at earlier. Remember that if something is purchased and not paid for immediately we call the supplier a trade creditor. Pause for a minute and have a look at the new balance sheet in Table 3.2. Can you follow how the accounting equation has altered the statement?

Table 3.2 Kitlocker Balance Sheet Mark II

	£	£
Assets		
Non-current assets		
Property, plant and equipment		1800
Current Assets		
Inventories	1700	
Cash and cash equivalents	7500	
		9200
Total assets		11000
Equity and Liabilities		
Equity		9500
Non-current liabilities		
Current Liabilities		
Trade and other payables		1500
Total equity and liabilities		11000

In this situation the supplier of the rugby jersyes will be recorded as a liability because when they are paid the business will be worth what it was originally. Let's see what happens when the supplier is paid in full.

$$£1,800 \text{ (FA, Machine)} + £6,000 \text{ (CA, Cash)} + £1,700 \text{ (CA, Stock)} = £9,500$$
$$\text{(Capital)} + £0 \text{ (Liabilities, Creditors)}$$

Before we move on from this there is one more transaction that it is worth looking at. Kitlocker purchased and eventually paid for 100 rugby jerseys in the above example. This was so that they could be sold to a university rugby team. As the company was established to make a profit a cash sale of the jerseys was made for £2,100. You can probably see that a profit of £600 was made on the original purchase but it is worth illustrating this in the accounting equation.

$$£1,800 \text{ (FA, Machine)} + £8,100 \text{ (CA, Cash)} + £200 \text{ (CA, Stock)} = £10,100$$
$$\text{(Capital)} + £0 \text{ (Liabilities, Creditors)}$$

In making the sale, the stock worth £1,500 was used up and cash of £2,100 received. You should note that the capital amount changes by the amount of profit (£600) generated in making the sale. The rough balance sheet would now look something like Table 3.3. We'll come back to this soon.

Table 3.3 Kitlocker Balance Sheet Mark III

	£	£
Assets		
Non-current assets		
Property, plant and equipment		1800
Current Assets		
Inventories	200	
Cash and cash equivalents	8100	
		8300
Total assets		10100
Equity and Liabilities		
Equity		10100
Non-current liabilities		
Current Liabilities		
Trade and other payables		0
Total equity and liabilities		10100

THE DOUBLE ENTRY RULE

This is where financial accounting gets interesting (and logical!). You already know that accountants need to identify, collect, measure, record, summarise and communicate financial information, but as yet probably have no idea how they do it. This section will begin to address the issues from 'identification' through to the 'recording' of transactions. Furthermore, we are still not too concerned about numbers: if you can understand the concept at this stage in your studies you will find it easy to become proficient with the numbers when we start to play with some.

The 'double entry rule' is the method by which financial transactions are recorded. The rule reflects the dual nature of all business transactions. It also provides a way of checking that all transactions have been recorded correctly. This in turn can lead to controls being put in place within the business.

Information is collected and stored in a nominal ledger (generally referred to as 'accounts' which we will show you in a minute). This is an accounting record, which summarises the financial affairs of a business, and it will contain details of assets, liabilities, incomes and expenditures. The ledger will normally consist of a large number of different accounts, each having its own purpose or name. Examples of these accounts may include machinery (a fixed asset), stock (current assets), wages and salaries (an expense) and sales (an income). Each transaction will give rise to a *debit* entry and a *credit* entry in the relevant accounts. The manual way of recording information is based on 'T-accounts': one half of the T will be for debits (the left hand side) and the other half (which is the right hand side – see how logical this is!) is for credits. The easy way to remember which side is which is: 'cRedit' has the letter 'R' in it and therefore it is on the Right). Ledger accounts are just like T accounts: each one has a debit side and a credit side. An example is shown below.

Account Name (e.g. Machinery account)

Debit	Credit

At the top of the account will be its name. Underneath the name will be the 'T' format and will be made up of the left hand or *debit* side, and the right hand *credit* side. One side of each account is for increases and the other for decreases. The problem here for students and managers is normally, which is which? The answer will become simple if you understand the 'double entry rule' which is

INCREASES (+) in ASSETS and EXPENSES

DEBIT	CREDIT
HERE	

INCREASES (+) in LIABILITIES and CAPITAL

DEBIT	CREDIT
	HERE

It follows that DECREASES (–) to an account will be the reverse of the above.

DECREASES (–) in ASSETS and EXPENSES

DEBIT	CREDIT
	HERE

DECREASES (–) in LIABILITIES and CAPITAL

DEBIT	CREDIT
HERE	

Observing this rule means that a transaction should *always* be recorded on the debit side of one account and on the credit side of another. This will provide you with an arithmetic check on the accuracy of your records, as the total debits should always equal the total credits.

A tricky one that often causes problems for students is 'sales'. What do you think 'sales' are recorded as? Hopefully you said 'a credit'. You can think through the logic of this as: if you sell something, in return you will get cash (or the promise of cash later, i.e. a debtor), the increase in cash is a debit entry (an asset) and therefore to make things balance, the sale must be a credit entry. Another way of remembering the pattern to underpin the 'rule' is:

Assets and expenses are debit entries.

Sales and liabilities are credit entries.

See how easy accounting is! Let's have a look at an example of a business transaction for Kitlocker.

In the case study earlier where we played around with the accounting equation you saw how things changed for Kitlocker following the purchase of a laser cutting machine. If we apply the double entry rule we can see how the 'T' accounts can be constructed.

First, we need to establish what is going on. As the machine was paid for in cash it is fairly easy to see what is happening. There has been an increase in the value of assets (Machines) of £1,800 and a decrease in assets (Cash) of the same amount. Now that we know what the two parts of the transaction are we can safely apply the rule.

INCREASES (+) in ASSETS and EXPENSES

DEBIT	CREDIT
HERE	

And,

DECREASES (–) in ASSETS and EXPENSES

DEBIT	CREDIT
	HERE

So,

Machinery Account

DEBIT	CREDIT
1,800	

And,

Cash and Bank Account

DEBIT	CREDIT
	1,800

Hopefully you follow this. Don't worry if you are still unsure though as we will have many more examples in just a minute. However, before we go any further it's probably time for another terminology check.

INCOME

Simply, all money that is received or receivable to the business regardless of its source or purpose.

EXPENSES

Pretty much the reverse of income! All money spent in relation to the company's commercial activities.

APPLYING THE DOUBLE ENTRY RULE

Dealing with the mechanics of the process (including the numbers) will be a case of practice makes perfect. If you understand the concept, and don't get confused by the accounting terminology, the practical implementation of the rule should not cause you any worries. It is also worth including a reference point (an extra column) for each account so that we can cross reference transactions. To help you get to grips with this, the following examples will take you through some typical transactions for Kitlocker and illustrate the way in which the double entry rule is applied and used.

1   If a printing machine is bought in cash for £1,500 we need to work out which two items will be affected.

In this question the values for Machinery and Cash will change. Going on you should also have said that machinery increases while cash decreases. We can summarise this transaction as follows:

■   Machinery +£1,500
■   Cash –£1,500

We can now apply the double entry rule to construct the 'T' accounts. To do this we need to record the following;

■   £1,500 on the debit (left) side of the Machinery account. Remember that Machinery is an Asset and these are increasing.
■   £1,500 on the credit (right) side of the Cash account. Here the Asset of Cash is decreasing as a result of buying the printing machine.
■   If you haven't followed this have another look at the double entry rule.

The 'T' accounts will therefore look like this.

Machinery Account

DEBIT (£)	CREDIT (£)
1,500	

Cash and Bank Account

DEBIT (£)	CREDIT (£)
	1,500

2   The business sells £500 of goods on credit.

Again we need to work out what is going on here. There is a sale and a credit transaction, which means that cash has not been received for the goods yet.

■   Sales +£500
■   Trade Debtors +£500

The transaction will need to be recorded in the company 'T' accounts as follows;

- £500 on the debit (left) side of the Trade Debtors account. Trade Debtors are an Asset to the business and are increasing.
- £500 on the credit (right) side of the Sales account. The Income of Sales is being increased and therefore so will capital.

The 'T' accounts will therefore look like this.

Trade Debtors Account

DEBIT (£)	CREDIT (£)
500	

Sales Account

DEBIT (£)	CREDIT (£)
	500

You should note here that the transactions have been recorded on the correct sides of each account in accordance to the double entry rule so that for each recorded debit we have a corresponding credit. Moreover, you could include a reference column, which, in practice, can be used for recording a date or the name of the other account involved. This will simply help when we go back through the books to ensure that everything has been recorded properly.

ACTIVITY

Now it's your turn. See if you can construct the 'T' accounts for the next four transactions before looking at our workings. These are a continuation of the examples illustrated above.

3   The business buys a delivery van for £1,000 and pays for it in cash.

Here the Asset of Cash is being used to purchase the Asset of Motors. So debit Motors (+Asset) and credit Cash (−Asset).

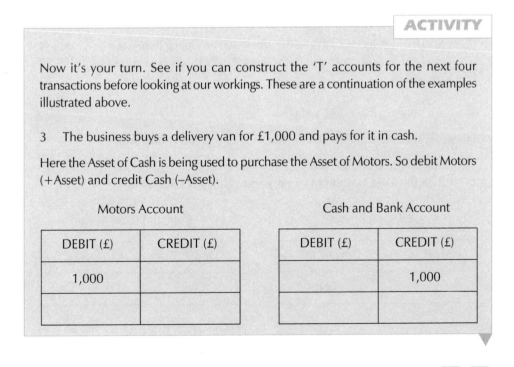

Motors Account

DEBIT (£)	CREDIT (£)
1,000	

Cash and Bank Account

DEBIT (£)	CREDIT (£)
	1,000

Happy? Try the next.

4 Goods for resale are purchased on credit from company X for £1,600.

Hopefully your answer looks something like this:

Purchases Account

DEBIT (£)	CREDIT (£)
1,600	

Trade Creditor X Account

DEBIT (£)	CREDIT (£)
	1,600

Did you get this correct? If not don't worry, as there are some important lessons here. First, it is important that purchases of stock and sales of stock are recorded in separate accounts as one is at cost price and the other is at selling price. This will help us to work out what profit was made on top of the purchase price. If you follow this logic then the account entries can be explained easily.

- Debit (left) side of the Purchases account (an Expense). Remember that it costs the business something before they can sell stock.
- Credit (right) side of the Trade Creditor X account as the trade creditors of the business have increased as they have not yet been paid. The business must acknowledge that they have to pay them back.
- We can assign individual creditors their own accounts; hence this one is called Trade Creditor X. This will help you to work through accounts with lots of transactions.

5 Cash sales are made of £3,600.

Hopefully this one was easy. If not check the double entry rule again.

- Debit the Cash and Bank account (+Asset) £3,600.
- Credit the Sales account (+Income and ultimately Capital).

Sales Account

DEBIT (£)	CREDIT (£)
	3,600

Cash and Bank Acount

DEBIT (£)	CREDIT (£)
3,600	

Note: you have sold goods and therefore the stock that you are holding will go down. Therefore there needs to be two more entries: credit the purchases account (by the amount the goods cost the business to buy, and debit 'cost of sales' account).

6   Wages of £200 are paid.

Wages Account

DEBIT (£)	CREDIT (£)
200	

Cash and Bank Account

DEBIT (£)	CREDIT (£)
	200

This transaction is an example of a bill being paid immediately. If the bill were not paid immediately it would go down on the trade creditor account. In these 'T' accounts we recorded the information this way because:

■   Wages are an expense so we record £200 on the debit (left) side.
■   Cash is a business asset and is used to pay the bill so the £200 is recorded on the credit (right) side.

Don't panic if you didn't follow how all of this worked. In the next chapter we will examine the routine policy decisions that managers make and how these are recorded in a company's 'T' accounts. However, the basic principles to work all of the information out are relatively straightforward. First, identify which two accounts are affected. Second, work out how they are affected e.g. increase/decrease, and third, apply the double entry rule.

What you are probably now wondering is where all of this is going and hopefully how we can use all of this information to develop company accounts. Simply, all of these accounts will need to be collated and checked for accuracy before the figures can be placed into the final accounts. The process for doing this is called a 'Trial Balance' – don't worry about this now though as we will look at it in Chapter 5.

SUMMARY

During this chapter you have seen the accounting system in practice. This is how accounting information is collected, recorded and summarised in its first stage. The examples from Kitlocker have illustrated how to keep 'T' accounts in good order and hopefully given you the basic skills needed to apply your knowledge to live situations. You must make sure that when you see transactions for a business you apply the double entry rule. If you do you will have a debit and credit entry for everything and will be well on the way to sorting out some final accounts. It is imperative that you understand these basic rules before you move on. We don't want to confuse you so have a go at the review questions and see where you are.

QUESTIONS FOR REVIEW

1   Complete the 'T' accounts for the following examples:

a The owner of the firm introduces capital of £15,000 in cash.

DEBIT (£)	CREDIT (£)		DEBIT (£)	CREDIT (£)

b Goods for re-sale are purchased, by cash, for £6,000.

DEBIT (£)	CREDIT (£)		DEBIT (£)	CREDIT (£)

c The rent bill arrives for the Gym amounting to £3,500.

DEBIT (£)	CREDIT (£)		DEBIT (£)	CREDIT (£)

d New machinery costing £10,000 is purchased for cash.

DEBIT (£)	CREDIT (£)

DEBIT (£)	CREDIT (£)

e Cash sales amount to £21,000.

DEBIT (£)	CREDIT (£)

DEBIT (£)	CREDIT (£)

f The business buys £5,000 of goods for re-sale on credit.

DEBIT (£)	CREDIT (£)

DEBIT (£)	CREDIT (£)

g New vehicles are bought for £30,000. A deposit of £13,000 is paid and the rest is put on credit.

DEBIT (£)	CREDIT (£)

DEBIT (£)	CREDIT (£)

2   Which of the following items are shown under the wrong headings?

Assets	Liabilities
Stock	Cash
Amounts due on stocks purchased	Amounts owing to creditors
Trade debtor	Mortgage
Bank overdraft	
Motor vehicle	

3   Complete the gaps in the table below.

	Assets	Liabilities	Capital
	£	£	£
(a)	16,200	8,500	?
(b)	21,000	?	11,075
(c)	?	4,560	18,790
(d)	12,350	?	8,000
(e)	65,800	?	55,000

1 Complete the 'T' accounts for the following examples:

a The owner of the firm introduces capital of £15,000 in cash.

Cash Account

DEBIT (£)	CREDIT (£)
15,000	

Capital Account

DEBIT (£)	CREDIT (£)
	15,000

b Goods for re-sale are purchased, by cash, for £6,000.

Purchases (Stock)

DEBIT (£)	CREDIT (£)
6,000	

Cash Account

DEBIT (£)	CREDIT (£)
	6,000

c The rent bill arrives for the Gym amounting to £3,500. Note the bill has not yet been paid.

Rent

DEBIT (£)	CREDIT (£)
3,500	

Trade Creditors

DEBIT (£)	CREDIT (£)
	3,500

61

d New machinery costing £10,000 is purchased for cash.

Machinery

DEBIT (£)	CREDIT (£)
10,000	

Cash Account

DEBIT (£)	CREDIT (£)
	10,000

e Cash sales amount to £21,000. Note we will deal with the reduction in stock later.

Sales

DEBIT (£)	CREDIT (£)
	21,000

Cash Account

DEBIT (£)	CREDIT (£)
21,000	

f The business buys £5,000 of goods for re-sale on credit.

Purchases (Stock)

DEBIT (£)	CREDIT (£)
5,000	

Trade Creditors

DEBIT (£)	CREDIT (£)
	5,000

g New vehicles are bought for £30,000. A deposit of £13,000 is paid and the rest is put on credit. Note, we have to record the full double entry here so need to split the asset up into two parts.

Motors

DEBIT (£)	CREDIT (£)
13,000	
17,000	

Cash Account

DEBIT (£)	CREDIT (£)
	13,000

Trade Creditors

DEBIT (£)	CREDIT (£)
	17,000

2 The following table illustrates where everything should go.

Assets	Liabilities
Stock	Bank overdraft
Cash	Amounts owing to creditors
Trade debtor	Mortgage
Motor vehicle	Amounts due on stocks purchased

3 Complete the gaps in the table below;

	Assets	Liabilities	Capital
	£	£	£
(a)	16,200	8,500	**7,700**
(b)	21,000	**9,925**	11,075
(c)	**23,350**	4,560	18,790
(d)	12,350	**4,350**	8,000
(e)	65,800	**10,800**	55,000

CHAPTER FOUR

ACCOUNTING RECORDS FOR SPORT AND LEISURE MANAGERS

On completion of this chapter you will be able to:

- Understand and communicate the impact of decisions and policies, and their effect on the financial statements.
- Apply common 'routine' transactions such as loan interest, depreciation, discounts, bad debts, returns and disposal of fixed assets.

INTRODUCTION

In this chapter we begin to bring together some of the principles that you covered in Chapters 2 and 3 where we looked at the basic format and contents of the accounts that are drawn up. The double entry system provides us with the 'technique' to record business transactions. You saw how it works in the real world when we looked at some typical trading transactions for Kitlocker. However, although you may well have followed the logic in some of our examples what you have seen so far is not a full view of the type of business transactions that you may come across. Therefore, we will use this chapter to cover some more 'common' transactions, and get you to apply your knowledge to record such transactions.

LOAN INTEREST

Businesses may take out loans to start the business, finance their operations or to expand. Unless the business has a generous benefactor, interest will have to be paid on the loans. A rate of interest will be agreed with the financier (usually a bank) and this will be charged on outstanding balances until the loan is repaid in full. The interest due will be calculated in reference to the amount borrowed and the rate of interest, and will be recorded in the accounts as an expense. For example, if a business takes out a loan of £10,000 at an interest rate of 6 per cent per year the interest expense for the first year will be £600 (£10,000 × 0.06).

Recording interest paid

Recording the interest paid is easy. All we need to do is open two accounts and follow the double entry rule. To illustrate, the interest in the example above will be recorded as follows: debit Interest Payable (+Expense), credit Cash and Bank (−Asset).

Interest Payable Account

DEBIT (£)	CREDIT (£)
600	

Cash and Bank Account

DEBIT (£)	CREDIT (£)
	600

You should note here that we have a debit and a credit entry so we have followed the double entry rule. However, there are a couple of points that you should always remember. First, interest must not be entered on the loan account itself, as the payment of interest does not represent a repayment of the loan (the amount borrowed). Second, interest paid (or payable) for the period will appear on the debit side of the Trial Balance, which we shall look at in Chapter 5, as it is a business expense. However, sometimes you may come across situations where the interest has been incurred but not paid. Can you remember what we do in this situation? If you said that it is an accrual then well done! Interest due at the end of an accounting period, but not yet paid, must be added to the interest paid account in order to account in full for the interest expense for that period. It must also be recorded as a liability (a trade creditor) because we have not paid the bill. Have a look at the example below to see how this works.

Example: Interest due but not yet paid

On the first day of an accounting period a business takes out a loan of £10,000 at an annual interest rate of 5 per cent. The terms of the loan are that repayments will be 'interest only'. This means that the annual amount of interest payable is £500 (£10,000 × 0.05). (*Note:* 'interest only' means that the annual payments will be just for the interest and the capital element of the loan will be paid off at an agreed date with one final payment. In this situation the amount of the loan will always be shown at the full amount until it is paid off.)

First we need to record the loan amount, so debit Cash and Bank £10,000 (+Asset) and credit Loans £10,000 (+Creditors).

During the year, £200 of the interest is paid, so debit Interest Paid £200 (+Expense) and credit Cash and Bank £200 (–Asset).

At the end of the year the outstanding interest must be recorded: it is an expense for that period. In practice the accounts are short of £300 (£500 – £200 = £300) of interest, so we need to debit Interest Paid £300 (+Expense) and credit Trade Creditors £300 (+Creditors). Consequently our 'T' accounts will look like this:

Cash and Bank Account

DEBIT (£)	CREDIT (£)
10,000	200

Interest Paid Account

DEBIT (£)	CREDIT (£)
200	
300	

Loans Account

DEBIT (£)	CREDIT (£)
	10,000

Trade Creditors Account

DEBIT (£)	CREDIT (£)
	300

When the final accounts are prepared for the year, the expense of 'interest paid' will be listed on the income statement (profit and loss account) as part of the calculation of profit. Loans will be recorded on the balance sheet under 'Non-current liabilities' (i.e. creditors payable after one year). However, the outstanding loan interest for the year will be part of the trade creditors that will be listed under 'Current liabilities' (i.e. creditors payable within one year).

It is important for you to realise that if payments are not made it will impact on the decisions and activities that the business can (or should!) make in the following accounting period. It is simple things like this that are often the reason for sport and leisure organisations losing control of their finances and facing growing debts.

1   What is the amount of interest payable for the year on a loan of £50,000 at an annual rate of interest of 7 per cent?
2   What is the percentage rate of interest per annum on a loan of £25,000 where the interest payable for the year is £1,250?
3   A business takes out a 5-year 'interest only' loan of £250,000, at an interest rate of 4 per cent per annum.

  ▪ Calculate the interest payable in the third year of the loan.
  ▪ What is the balance on the loan account at the end of the third year.

Answers

1   £3,500 (£50,000 × 0.07 = £3,500).
2   5 per cent (£1,250/25,000 = 0.05, × 100 = 5%)
3   £10,000 (£250,000 × 0.04 = £10,000) and £250,000 (the capital will not be paid off until the agreed final date).

The above examples illustrate how to record the transactions for simple 'interest only' loans. The same pattern should be used when recording the transactions that arise with other loans. In reality, lenders are more likely to want some of the capital sum to be repaid each year. An example of how this would be recorded follows.

The annual repayments on a five-year £12,000 loan at 10 per cent per annum would be £3,165. The mechanics of the loan would be:

▪   When taking out the loan, the entries would be the same as before: debit 'bank' (or cash) and credit 'loan' with the capital sum (in this case £12,000).
▪   Year 1: the interest would be £1,200 (calculated as 10 per cent of £12,000). This means that £1,965 is paid off the capital (£3,165 – £1,200). The financial statements at the end of the year will show 'interest paid' of £1,200 and a loan of £10,035.
▪   Year 2: the interest would be £1,004 (calculated as 10 per cent of the outstanding loan of £10,035). This means that £2,161 is paid off the loan. The financial statements at the end of the year will show 'interest paid' of £1,004 and a loan of £7,874.
▪   Years 3, 4 and 5 will follow the same pattern. After the payment at the end of the fifth year the balance on the loan will be zero. Please work through the numbers for years 3, 4, and 5 to prove to yourself that it works (with a small rounding factor!).

DEPRECIATION

Many businesses will purchase fixed assets such as machines, motor vehicles etc. for use within the business. Such fixed assets will normally be used for more than one accounting period. This causes a problem: the asset has been bought and consequently recorded in the accounts of one year but will serve the business for more than one year. It would not be 'fair' to charge the income statement with all of the cost of the asset in the first year of ownership: the business will receive the benefits of owning the asset for future years too. If we charged the full amount in the year that we acquired the asset we would distort the income statement: too much expense would be charged in the first year and the later years would not have any expense. This contravenes the matching concept: income and related expenses must be matched with each other. Also it is unrealistic not to charge any expense in any of the years: this would mean that the asset would continue to be valued at its purchase price on the balance sheet (this is not logical: the value will reduce because of usage, wear and tear etc.).

For example, at the beginning of year 1 a business buys a printing machine for £5,000 cash. The business estimates that it will be able to use the asset for 5 years but then it will have to be replaced and have no scrap value. Therefore we need to charge each of the five years with some of the cost of the machine. The resulting charge is called 'depreciation' and given that it as an 'expense' it must be charged against income for each year and as a reduction in the value of the fixed asset. This follows the 'double entry rule': we will debit an expense and the opposite credit value will be to an account 'Provision for depreciation'. At the end of the year the balance sheet will show the asset at £5,000 less £1,000 depreciation. The resulting balance of £4,000 is known as the 'net book value' (cost less accumulated depreciation). In the second year, another £1,000 will be charged to the income statement for year 2 and the balance sheet for that year will show the asset as having a net book value of £3,000. Depreciation is the accounting entry made to share the cost of an asset over its life.

Important! It is very important that you realise what is happening to cash here. Depreciation has got nothing to do with cash flow. If a business buys an asset for cash, the cash will leave the business on the day that the asset is purchased. Or if a loan is arranged to buy the asset, the cash leaves on the days the repayments are due. Depreciation is not a cash flow. This is one of the reasons why 'profit' is not 'cash': a business may show that it has made a profit in the income statement but it does not mean that it has got cash.

Recording depreciation

If we stick with our printing machines example we can illustrate the recording of depreciation in the 'T' accounts. Most businesses assume that the depreciation will be spread equally over the life of the asset. This makes our job much easier! The method for doing this is called 'Straight Line Depreciation' and it is very simple. To work out the depreciation for our machine all we do is divide the value by the number of useful years (£5,000/5). This means that our annual depreciation charge will be £1,000.

The entries in the 'T' accounts are also simple when we use the double entry rule. First, open the necessary accounts and record the acquisition of the machine. Debit Machinery at Cost £5,000 (+Asset) and credit Cash and Bank £5,000 (–Asset): remember you have used one asset to get another. Second,we need to record the depreciation so, debit Depreciation Expense £1,000 (+Expense) and credit Provision for Depreciation of Machinery £1,000 (+Provision). Having done this our 'T' accounts will look like this:

Cash and Bank Account

DEBIT (£)	CREDIT (£)
	5,000

Machinery at Cost Account

DEBIT (£)	CREDIT (£)
5,000	

Depreciation Expense Account

DEBIT (£)	CREDIT (£)
1,000	

Provision for Depreciation of Machinery Account

DEBIT (£)	CREDIT (£)
	1,000

As with the loan interest example when the final accounts are prepared the depreciation expense will be recorded on the income statement as an expense so that net profit can be calculated. The balances remaining on the Machinery at Cost account and on the Provision of Depreciation of Machinery account will appear on the balance sheet. In this example our machine will have a net book value of £4,000 (£5,000 – £1,000). The balance on the provision account should increase each year so that by the end of year 5 it is worth £5,000 whereas the Machinery at Cost is £0.

ACTIVITIES

Assume Kitlocker is expanding and it needs to purchase an embroidery machine costing £20,000. They estimate that the machine will have a useful life of eight years after which time the item will have no scrap value. Kitlocker uses the straight-line method of depreciation.

70

1   How much is the depreciation charge per annum?
2   What will be the annual percentage rate of depreciation?
3   What will be the balance on the Provision for Depreciation of Machinery account at the end of year 4?
4   What will the net book value of the machine be at the end of year 6?

Answers

1   £2,500 (£20,000/8 = £2,500).
2   12.5 per cent (£2,500/20,000 = 0.125 ×100 = 12.5 per cent).
3   £10,000 (£2,500 × 4 = £10,000).
4   £5,000 (£20,000 – (£2,500 × 6) = £5,000).

Depreciation adjustments

Generally the recording of depreciation is straightforward and most students will understand how to perform the calculations after a bit of practice. However, one of the areas that seem to cause trouble for students is making depreciation adjustments.

Depreciation allocates part of the cost of a fixed asset as an expense to the income statement (in order to match the use of the assets through its estimated useful life). However, in reality estimates are rarely 100 per cent accurate. An asset may well be used beyond the end of its original estimated useful life (for example, if it has been well maintained) and conversely it may become useless before originally thought. To account for the change in the profile of the asset it is necessary to make a one-off adjustment to the depreciation provision to reflect a change of circumstance.

Making the adjustment is itself fairly easy providing that you understand whether the Provision for Depreciation account needs to be increased or reduced – this is normally the first troublesome issue for students – a corresponding entry needs to be made in the Depreciation Expense account. Can you remember how depreciation was recorded earlier? To remind you the two entries needed are: debit Depreciation Expense account (+Expense) and credit the Provision for Depreciation account (+Provision).

Consequently if we decide that the balance on the Provision for Depreciation is too low, i.e. the asset will not be useful for as long as we originally thought, an additional amount must be debited to the Depreciation Expense account and credited to the Provision for Depreciation account. Alternatively if we think that the asset will be useful for longer than originally thought, we need to raise the balance on the Depreciation Provision account by recording a credit on the Depreciation Expense account and a debit on the Provision for Depreciation account. Get it? Don't worry if you don't, we'll look at an example.

Example: Depreciation adjustment

Kitlocker decides to purchase a new computer, for £2,000, to help design kit logos. They expect to be able to use the computer for 5 years. Therefore, using the straight-line method for depreciation, the depreciation charge will be £400 per year (£2,000/5). At the end of year 3, the computer will have a net book value of £800. However, during a financial review, it is decided that due to advances in technology the computer will become useless at the end of year 4. An adjustment needs to be made to the Provision for Depreciation Account as follows.

First we need to work out what the adjustment is:

Annual Depreciation based on a life of 3 years (not 5)	= £500 (£2,000/4)
Accumulated depreciation to the end of year 3	= £1,500 (£500 × 3years)
Accumulated depreciation already provided	= £1,200
Adjustment or extra depreciation needed	= £300 (£1,500 – £1,200)

The rest is easy, thanks to the double entry rule. Our entries will be: debit Depreciation Expense £300 (+Expense) and credit Provision for Depreciation £300 (+Provision). It is important to also note here that as a result of the extra depreciation profit will decrease by £300. The 'T' accounts will look like this.

Depreciation Expense Account

DEBIT (£)	CREDIT (£)
1200	
300	

Provision for Depreciation of Machinery Account

DEBIT (£)	CREDIT (£)
	1200
	300

DISCOUNTS

If you think back to Chapter 3 where you were introduced to Kitlocker and some of its transactions you may have noticed that they purchased and sold stock on credit terms, hence we used the Trade Creditor and Trade Debtor accounts regularly. This is a very common situation: many businesses buy and sell goods on credit terms. It may be several weeks before bills are finally settled. This arrangement can be useful to businesses and their customers as it offers a good incentive to buy and sell. However, as we have mentioned throughout this book, a business is measured on its ability to pay debts as they fall due. Consequently, getting money from customers and paying creditors is very important.

Discounts allowed

In order for Kitlocker to collect cash from its customers (debtors) as quickly as possible they may offer a discount for prompt payment. When this situation occurs the business will receive less money than it had originally hoped for. The difference, or discount allowed, must be recognised as a business expense. For example, Kitlocker sold goods to a regular customer for £500. The customer is told that they will receive a 5 per cent discount if payment is received within 10 working days. The necessary entries will be as follows. First ignore the discount and record the sale, so, debit Trade Debtors £500 (+Asset) and credit Sales (+Income). Next, the debtor pays immediately so we need to record the settlement. Debit Cash and Bank £475 (£500 – 5%) (+Asset), credit Trade Debtors £475 (–Asset). Kitlocker agrees the discount of £25 so, debit Discount Allowed £25 (+Expense) and credit Trade Debtors (–Asset).

The 'T' accounts are illustrated below but you should also note that the discount allowed reduces the Asset of debtors and not the sales income. When the final accounts are prepared the sales figure will go to the Income section of the income statement and the discount allowed to the Expense section.

Sales Account

DEBIT (£)	CREDIT (£)
	500

Cash and Bank Account

DEBIT (£)	CREDIT (£)
	475

Trade Debtors Account

DEBIT (£)	CREDIT (£)
500	475
	25

Discount Allowed Account

DEBIT (£)	CREDIT (£)
25	

Discounts received

While we are talking about discounts it is also worth noting that they can work in favour of Kitlocker. Remember that it purchased some of its goods on credit and as such Kitlocker will be recorded as a trade debtor in the books of its suppliers. They will have many suppliers that will want payment as soon as possible and as such will offer them a discount to pay early. When a business like Kitlocker deducts discount from the amount owed to its trade creditors, the cash paid will be lower than the amount being settled. The difference, or discount received, can therefore be treated as income. Again we can have a quick look at an example.

Kitlocker purchased 200 rugby jerseys from one of its regular suppliers for £1,000. It will receive an 8 per cent discount if it can make the payment in 21 days. The entries will mirror what we did with discount allowed with two notable exceptions – can you spot them? First we can ignore the discount and record the purchase of the goods so, debit Purchases £1,000 (+Expense) and credit trade creditors £1,000 (+Creditors). Kitlocker then pays within the 21 days, so, we debit Trade Creditors £920 (£1,000 – 8%) (–Creditors) and credit Cash and Bank £920 (–Asset). Finally, Kitlocker claims the discount and debits Trade Creditors £80 (–Creditors) and credits Discount Received £80 (+Income). Discounts received reduce the amount of creditors and not the purchases as when the final accounts are prepared the purchases figure is used to calculate the cost of sales figure (which we shall look at later). Discount received is treated as income in the income statement.

Before you look at the 'T' accounts illustrated below, did you spot the two differences? If you said that two of the accounts were different – well done. Here we use Purchases instead of Sales, and Trade Creditors instead of Trade Debtors.

Purchases Account

DEBIT (£)	CREDIT (£)
1000	

Cash and Bank Account

DEBIT (£)	CREDIT (£)
	920

Trade Creditors Account

DEBIT (£)	CREDIT (£)
920	1000
80	

Discount Received Account

DEBIT (£)	CREDIT (£)
	80

ACTIVITIES

One of Kitlocker's trade creditors is owed £5,000. The supplier has arranged for a discount of 10 per cent to be deducted if Kitlocker pays within 14 days. Assuming that payment is made within 14 days can you answer the following?

74

1   Will this be 'discount allowed' or 'discount received' in Kitlocker's accounts?
2   What is the amount of the discount?
3   What accounting entries will be required to record the discounted payment (ignore the original purchase)?
4   What impact will the discount have on the profit on the period?

Answers

1   Discount received.
2   £500 (£5,000 × 0.1 = £500).
3   Debit Trade Creditors £4,500, Credit Cash and Bank £4,500, Debit Trade Creditors £500 and Credit Discount Received £500.
4   Profit will increase by the £500 discount received.

BAD DEBTS

In the previous section you will have seen one of the strategies that businesses use in an attempt to recoup money that is owed to them. For the most part customers will pay you what they owe but there will be examples where a debt 'goes bad' and is not paid. The offering of credit terms will usually be an incentive for customers to trade with you, however, it must be noted that there is always a risk that some of your debtors may not pay up. You have to recognise here that when a debt goes bad it can no longer be viewed as an asset (remember that when a sale is made on credit the trade debtors (assets) of the business go up). Therefore, a bad debt must be recorded as an expense. As usual an example is the best way to see how this works in practice.

Example: Recording bad debts

Assume that Kitlocker has recently sold a team volleyball kit to a local team. The sale of £1,500 was made on credit terms. First they need to recognise the sale so they debit Trade Debtors £1,500 (+Asset) and credit Sales £1,500 (+Income). However, the team is declared bankrupt and cannot pay its debt to the company. If you remember that a bad debt reduces the asset of debtors, not income, the double entry is quite easy. Although Kitlocker doesn't necessarily want to, it is forced to write off the £1,500 as a bad debt. The entries are: debit Bad Debt Expense (+Expense) and credit Trade Debtors (–Asset). When the final accounts are prepared the sales figure is transferred to the income statement as Income and the Bad Debt Expense to Expenses. It is also worth noting here that the Trade Debtors account, on the balance sheet, must not include any bad debts. The 'T' accounts are shown below.

75

Sales Account

DEBIT (£)	CREDIT (£)
	1,500

Trade Debtors Account

DEBIT (£)	CREDIT (£)
1,500	
	1,500

Cash and Bank Account

DEBIT (£)	CREDIT (£)
1,500	

As a manager or potential manager you should note here the dangers of offering credit facilities. Kitlocker, as a relatively new business, would need to break into new markets and therefore offered credit facilities and discounts as incentives to customers. However, you should always seek to establish the credit worthiness of a business before trading in this way. Furthermore, you should make every effort to recover debts, even if just in part. Writing off transactions as bad debts should be a last resort.

Provision for bad debts

Some businesses will set-up a 'provision for bad debts' just in case anything goes wrong with their debtors. Such provision will be necessary if it is considered that there may be doubtful debts contained in the Trade Debtors figure (remember that final accounts have to give a true and fair view). The creation of these provision accounts follows much the same logic as the provision for depreciation. By making the provision of bad debts account we are able to reduce the Debtors figure on the balance sheet in accordance with the prudence concept, which states that revenues and profits should only be recognised when they are realised.

For example, if Kitlocker sold various team kits to credit customers for £10,000 it would have debited Trade Debtors £10,000 and credited Sales £10,000. However, if we look back on the previous example we saw that debtors worth £1,500 went bad and were written off by debiting Bad Debt Expense £1,500 and crediting Trade Debtors £1,500. Following this Kitlocker approached some of its other customers to ask for payment to avoid a similar situation. Consequently, debtors worth £6,000 paid up. Kitlocker was then able to debit 'Cash and Bank' £6,000 and credit 'Trade Debtors' £6,000. This left a balance of £2,500 on its Trade Debtors account. At the end of the accounting period the existing debtors were evaluated and it was decided that 5 per cent of the remaining debt may be bad i.e. £125 (£2,500 × 5%). It was decided to make a provision to cover this and debit Bad Debt Expense £125 (+Expense) and credit Provision for Bad Debts £125 (+Provision). The ledger accounts looked like this;

Sales Account

DEBIT (£)	CREDIT (£)
	10,000

Trade Debtors Account

DEBIT (£)	CREDIT (£)
10,000	1,500
	6,000

Bad Debt Expense Account

DEBIT (£)	CREDIT (£)
1,500	
125	

Cash and Bank Account

DEBIT (£)	CREDIT (£)
6,000	

Provision for Bad Debt Account

DEBIT (£)	CREDIT (£)
	125

You should probably note here that the purpose of having a provision for bad debts account is purely to provide an amount, which will reduce the asset of trade debtors (much like the depreciation exercise) on the balance sheet to net realisable value (in other words the balance sheet is showing the amount of money that you expect to be paid). This is achieved by subtracting the balance on the provision for bad debts account from the balance on the trade debtor's account. If you are required to make any adjustments you can follow the same stages as you did to adjust depreciation. For example if it is thought that more customers will default on their debts it will be necessary to change the provision for bad debts to a higher percentage. The value of the change would be shown as an extra expense in the income statement and the revised provision would be used to reduce the value of the debtors shown in the balance sheet.

As a manager you should be careful in your treatment of credit and bad debts. It may well be your responsibility to provide a detailed analysis of customers so that you can decide whether credit options should be given. This information can then be used to decide how to manage the recovery of outstanding debt and to calculate a realistic provision for bad debts.

RETURNS

In business there may be times when goods will have to be returned to a supplier. Consider how many times you have had to take things back to shops! What do you think happens to the goods that you return? If they are just wrong for you then they may well go back onto the shelf, however, if they are faulty, chances are that they will be sent back to the supplier. You may have noticed that there are actually two things going on here. First, you have the customer return, for example the football boots that you have returned because the soles came apart – we call this a return of sale or returns inwards. Second, you have the return of goods to the supplier, that is the return of the faulty football boots to the manufacturer – we call this a return of purchase or returns outwards.

Returns inwards

If a customer returns goods (for example football boots back to a shop) the shop accounts must show a decrease in sales and a decrease in cash (if a cash refund is given immediately) or a decrease in trade debtors (if there is no immediate cash refund). Note that these two 'decreases' balance each other off because one is a debit and the other is a credit.

The sale of the boots caused the accounting entries debit 'Cost of sales' and credit 'Inventory'. The return of the boots means that the entries now have to be reversed to cancel out the previous ones (we now credit 'Cost of sales' and debit 'Inventory').

Returns outwards

Just like returns inwards, returns outwards are easy to record. When purchases are returned to a supplier (football boots back to the manufacturer) the accounts must show a decrease in purchases (or Inventory) and an increase in cash (providing a cash refund is obtained immediately) or a decrease in trade creditors (if there is no immediate cash refund). Again this is simple to record. If a cash refund is obtained immediately then a company will debit cash and bank (+Asset) and credit purchases (−Expense) and if a cash refund is not obtained immediately they debit trade creditors (−Creditors) and credit purchases (−Expense).

Consider the following questions for Kitlocker.
What accounting entries will the company need if:

1   Customers return goods and obtain a cash refund immediately?
2   The company returns goods to one of its suppliers and receives a credit note (i.e. does not obtain a cash refund)?

Answers

1   Debit 'Sales' and credit 'Cash and Bank' with the sales value of the goods, and debit 'Inventory' and credit 'Cost of sales' with the price Kitlocker paid for the goods.
2   Debit 'Trade Creditors', and credit 'Purchases' or 'Inventory'.

DISPOSALS OF FIXED ASSETS

If you think back to Chapter 2 where you were introduced to assets and in particular fixed assets you may have thought that accounting for bringing them into the business is all very well but what happens if and when you dispose of them. Indeed earlier in this chapter when we considered depreciation you may have wondered why a company would keep assets until they were worthless – why not sell them while they still had some value? Here we will deal with those questions and show you how it can be done and how it should be recorded.

You are aware that fixed assets are used by a business so that it can carry out its business (the fixed assets are not for trade – they are used to enable trade to take place). The assets will last for more than one accounting period but their value will depreciate over time. However, before the end of an asset's useful life it can and probably will be sold (the company may need more efficient machinery in order to remain, or become, competitive). Occasionally an asset may be sold for its net book value (NBV) (cost – depreciation) but given that the depreciation charge is only an estimate, it is more likely that the net book value and the sale proceeds are two different figures!

Example: Asset disposal

When Kitlocker was established in 2005 a van was purchased for £1,000. This van has been depreciated by 25 per cent per year on cost meaning that the NBV of the van at the end of year 1 is £750. Immediately after the end of the first year Kitlocker decided to get a better van. The old van was sold for £600. Clearly there is a 'loss' of £150 (the business valued the van at £750 but it only realised £600) and it is important that this, and the associated transactions, are dealt with in the income statement for year 2 so that the accounts show a true and fair view.

In order to make the necessary entries in the company's 'T' accounts a number of stages have to be followed. We'll need to open some new accounts that are unfamiliar to you so that we can record the sale of the van (so take your time when reading this and then you will appreciate the logic). First, the company needs to identify the original cost of the vehicle being sold (£1,000) and transfer this to the Disposal account. To do this they debit the disposal account £1,000 (+Expense) and credit Vehicles at Cost £1,000 (–Asset).

Second, the company needs to calculate the accumulated depreciation provided on the asset being sold: in this case it is only one year's worth (£250). This figure is transferred to the Disposals account using the following entries: debit Provision for Depreciation of Vehicles account £250 and credit Disposals account £250. At this stage the balance on the Disposals account represents the net book value of the vehicle, i.e. £750.

Finally the sale of the asset needs to be recorded. We can assume that the cash is paid immediately so the entries will be: debit Cash £600 and credit Disposals account £600. The balance on the disposals account will now represent the profit or loss on the disposal. You should also note here that for each stage of the transaction the disposals account is used. Ultimately the 'T' accounts will look like this:

Vehicles at Cost Account

DEBIT (£)	CREDIT (£)
	1,000

Provision for Depreciation of Vehicles Account

DEBIT (£)	CREDIT (£)
250	

Disposals Account

DEBIT (£)	CREDIT (£)
1,000	250
	600

Cash and Bank Account

DEBIT (£)	CREDIT (£)
600	

In this example, when we balance off the accounts there will be a debit balance of £150 on the disposals account which will be transferred to the expense section of the income statement which will reduce any profit by £150.

Assume that Kitlocker purchases a new embroidery machine that will allow it to produce team kit with stitched logos and names. The machine costs the business £15,000 and should have a useful life of 10 years. They find out that the industry standard is to depreciate the equipment by 12 per cent per annum on cost.

1 What will be the annual depreciation charge for the machine? (Assume the straight line method for depreciation.)
2 What will be the accumulated depreciation by the end of year 5?
3 What will be the NBV of the machine at the end of year 5?
4 At the end of year 6 the company decides to sell the machine for £3,000. What is the profit/loss for the machine?
5 What are the accounting entries for question 4?

Answers

1 £1,500 (£15,000/10 = £1,500).
2 £7,500 (£1,500 × 5 = £7,500).
3 £7,500 (£15,000 − £7,500 = £7,500).
4 Loss on disposal is £3,000 (NBV end of year 6 = £15,000 − (£1,500 × 6) = £6,000. Therefore Loss on disposal = £6,000 − £3,000 = £3,000).
5 a Debit Disposals a/c £15,000, credit Machinery at Cost a/c £15,000.
  b Debit Provision for Depreciation of Machinery £9,000, credit Disposals a/c £9,000.
  c Debit Cash and Bank £3,000, credit Disposals a/c £3,000.

SUMMARY

The aim of this chapter was to introduce you to the common routine decisions and transactions that sport and leisure managers make on a regular basis. It is important that you understand how these actions are recorded in the company accounts so that you can begin to see the consequences of their (and soon, *your*) decisions. Obtaining loan finance, giving trade and cash discounts, offering credit facilities, returning goods and disposing of assets will all have an impact on the running, and finances, of the business.

1   What is the net book value of an asset?
2   A machine cost £50,000 and was being depreciated at 20 per cent per annum. If the depreciation rate was changed to 25 per cent per year, how much extra cash would leave the company in the second year of the machine's usage?
3   Would 'interest receivable' be shown as an expense?
4   Explain the difference between 'interest payments' and 'capital repayments' on a loan.
5   Would 'discounts allowed' be shown as an expense?

1   It is the residue of the cost of the asset minus the depreciation to date. Note we have called it a residue because we can't find a good word to describe it because it is not a 'real' item: it is cash (the purchase price of the asset) less an accounting estimate (a figure used to match a share of the value of the asset to the periods it was used in). The net book value is not what you can sell the asset for!

2   There is no change: depreciation is not cash!

3   Interest receivable is the amount of interest that an organisation would receive. Monies received are income and not expenses. Interest payable is an expense.

4   Interest payments are payments for the interest on a loan: the interest accrues on the amount of the loan outstanding (the capital). Capital payments are payments that reduce the amount of capital outstanding.

5   Yes: discounts are allowed as an expense.

CHAPTER FIVE

THE INTERRELATIONSHIP BETWEEN 'T' ACCOUNTS AND FINAL STATEMENTS

On completion of this chapter you will be able to:

- Understand and communicate the interrelationship between 'T' accounts and financial statements.
- Determine balances on 'T' accounts and construct a trial balance.
- Construct an outline income statement and balance sheet.

INTRODUCTION

By now you should understand the rules that govern how and why ledger accounts are constructed. Hopefully you have now begun to wonder how all of this information will ultimately be recorded in a set of final accounts (like the ones that we saw illustrated back in Chapters 1 and 2). Remember that the details of all transactions for a business are recorded in the appropriate 'T' accounts as and when they occur. Before we use them to construct the final accounts, however, it is necessary to make sure that they are correct. We can test the arithmetic accuracy of the accounts by constructing a trial balance; this merely involves listing and then totalling, separately, the credit and debit balances (we told you there is no need to be a skilled mathematician to understand accounts!). The trial balance is the second step in the production of the final accounts.

TRIAL BALANCE

This is simply a list of nominal ledger ('T') account balances. It is used primarily as a measure to see if credit balances equal debit balances. Ultimately it will offer some reassurance that the double entry rule has been applied correctly.

Nearly all of the information that you need to draw up an income statement (Profit and Loss account) can be found in the trial balance. All you need to do is pick the right figures. The balance sheet is formulated in a very similar way too. However, you will need to make certain adjustments to the basic information held in the trial balance before we can work out profit values etc. Chapter 2 outlined the fundamental rules and now we have to apply them to ensure that when we come out with a set of final figures they represent a true and fair view. Later chapters will cover the key adjustments that you need to be aware of, and show you how to perform the calculations. However, before we do this we need to cover the trial balance.

THE TRIAL BALANCE

It is very important that when recording the transactions in the ledgers that you have some sort of control system to check the 'accuracy' of what has been done. One of these controls, which also serves as an arithmetic check, is the trial balance. In this section we will outline the guiding principles of constructing one. You will need to apply this knowledge in later chapters (so it is important that you understand what is happening as we go along).

As each transaction involves a debit entry and a credit entry of the same value, it will follow that if we add up all of the debits they should equal the total of all of the credits. The aim therefore of the trial balance is to prove that for every debit entry a balancing credit entry has been made.

As one side of each individual 'T' account records increases and the other records decrease the difference between the two sides will represent the net value, or balance, of that account. For example, if total cash receipts amount to £25,000 and total cash payments total £15,000 the value, or balance, of the cash account will be £10,000. By balancing off the account we can simplify the account so that only one figure is carried forward to the final accounts. Below you can see how this balancing off process works in practice.

1   Leaving a line blank, rule a total box on each side of the account. The total boxes must be level with each other. This is demonstrated by the Cash & Bank Account below.

Cash and Bank Account

	DEBIT	(£)		CREDIT	(£)
Jan 1	Capital	15,000	Jan 2	Motors	5,000
6	Sales	6,750	9	Purchases	3,250
18	T. Debtors	3,250	19	Wages	750
			29	T. Creditors	6,000
	(Total Box)				

2   Add up the debit side of the account (= £25,000).
3   Add up the credit side of the account (= £15,000).
4   Enter the *greater* value in *each* total box (= £25,000).
5   Enter the shortfall – the closing balance to be carried down ('c/d') of £10,000 – to the credit side to make both sides equal.
6   The balance must be brought down ('b/d') on the *opposite* side (the debit side), *below* the total box.

Cash and Bank Account

	DEBIT	(£)		CREDIT	(£)
Jan 1	Capital	15,000	Jan 2	Motors	5,000
6	Sales	6,750	9	Purchases	3,250
18	T. Debtors	3,250	19	Wages	750
			29	T. Creditors	6,000
			Jan 31	**Balance c/d**	**10,000**
	(Total Box)	**25,000**			**25,000**
Feb 1	**Balance b/d**	**10,000**			

'T' accounts and final statements

Please note:

- The balancing off of the account has netted the total value of all the entries on the account for the period.
- As the debit side exceeded the credit side, the balance of £10,000 is a debit balance, i.e. a net debit.
- The cash transactions for the next period will be entered as debits and credits below the ruled off total box and the brought down entry.
- According to the Cash & Bank Account, there is £10,000 available at the end of the period/beginning of the next period, i.e. 31 Jan/1 Feb.
- At the end of the year the final 'T' accounts will be balanced off and their values used for the final accounts.

That should have been relatively straightforward. However, let's see if you can put it into practice by answering the following questions. Draw out each of the 'T' accounts on paper and balance them all off. If it makes it easier, pretend that the transactions relate to Kitlocker.

ACTIVITY

Mike sets up a company to sell sports kit to University sport teams. He puts £7,000 of his own money into the business and in the first period of trading the following transactions occurred.

1 Mike introduces £7,000 of cash into the business as capital.
2 Rent is paid, by cash, on the shop of £3,500 for the period.
3 Clothing for resale costing £5,000 is purchased on credit.
4 The company takes out a bank loan for £1,000.
5 Shop fittings are purchased for cash of £2,000.
6 A university team is signed and the company makes sales of £10,000 for cash.
7 Some more goods are sold, this time on credit, for £2,500.
8 Trade creditors are paid, by cash, £4,250.
9 Trade debtors pay £1,500.
10 Interest on the business loan is paid totalling £100.
11 Administration costs of £100 are paid for in cash.
12 Mike makes drawings of £1,500.

Answers are given at the end of the chapter.

Once you have completed the 'T' account entries balance off each account and record the balances in a Trial Balance.

88

Hopefully it should look something like this (don't worry if things are in a different order).

	Debit (£)	Credit (£)
Cash	8,050	
Capital		7,000
Bank Loan		1,000
Stock (purchases)	5,000	
Trade Creditors		750
Rent	3,500	
Shop Fittings	2,000	
Sales		12,500
Trade Debtors	1,000	
Loan Interest	100	
Administration Expenses	100	
Drawings	1,500	
	21,250	21,250

If yours is slightly different, or if the debits do not equal the credits, go back through your accounts and check them against the double entry rule. It may help if you work out the difference first as you may have only made one error. However, before you start your trawl, check the list of common errors below.

1 Is there a complete omission of a transaction?
2 Have you posted something to the wrong account?
3 Have you recorded a credit when you should have recorded a debit?
4 Are there more debits than credits (or vice versa)? Have you followed the double entry rule?

In our example there was actually very little balancing to do. Only the cash account and sales account had some real activity with the remaining ones just having one or two transactions. If you've really got into a mess have a look at our 'T' accounts, which you can find after the review questions at the end of the chapter.

You shouldn't worry if your trial balance has been prepared in a different order than ours as it is not a published document like the balance sheet and income statement. It is, as the key term above suggests, just a method to test the accuracy of your double entry bookkeeping.

LIMITATIONS TO THE TRIAL BALANCE

Obviously if the debit column and credit columns do not balance you have made an error in your application of the double entry rule. However, you need to be aware that the trial balance is not a perfect measurement tool. It too has its limitations due to its inability to uncover the following errors.

- An error of omission – if there is a total omission of a transaction, the trial balance may still balance (providing there are no other mistakes). For example, in the activity above there would have been no quick way of knowing that you had forgotten to record the details of the rent.
- An error of commission – you may post a transaction to the wrong account while choosing the right type of account. For example, you may post something to the telephone account when you should have posted it to the rent account.
- Compensating errors – these occur when one error is cancelled by another.
- Errors of principle – transactions are posted to the wrong account, for example you post something to motor expenses rather than fixed assets.
- Errors of original entry – the wrong amount is debited and credited to the correct accounts. You should probably note that this is also one of the most common yet basic errors in student work!

THE TRIAL BALANCE BALANCES! NOW WHAT?

Now it's time to start thinking about the two major financial statements; the income statement and balance sheet. These are designed to provide the users of accounting information with a picture of the overall financial position and performance of the business. Providing that the trial balance has been produced and we have been reassured that the double entry rule has been applied correctly the next step in preparing the financial statements is to produce a trading income statement and balance sheet. These 'trading' statements are not the final statements that we are looking for but they will give us an early picture of what needs to be completed before we produce them.

The first step that you need to take when doing this is to identify which accounts feed into the income statement and which feed into the balance sheet. At this point it is probably worth reminding you what each of the main statements is for as you need to be able to put the trial balance into context and we shall be using the two statements more regularly from now on.

PROFT AND LOSS ACOUNT

The profit and loss account (income statement) is a statement showing the profits (or losses) recognised during a period. The profit is calculated by deducting expenditure (including charges for capital maintenance) from income.

BALANCE SHEET

The balance sheet is a list of all of the assets owned by a business and all of the liabilities owed by a business at a specific point in time. It is often referred to as a 'snapshot' of the financial position of the business at a specific moment in time (the end of the financial year).

With these definitions in mind we can begin to identify which accounts will feed into which statement. For example, in the activity above Mike had to pay a rent bill of £3,500. If you accounted for it correctly you will have noticed that it is an expense and will therefore go on the income statement.

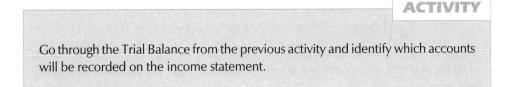

ACTIVITY

Go through the Trial Balance from the previous activity and identify which accounts will be recorded on the income statement.

A brief insight into the trading income statement

For the previous activity you should have been able to identify that the following accounts would be transferred to the trading income statement.

- Purchases (stock) £5,000 Debit
- Rent £3,500 Debit
- Loan Interest £100 Debit
- Administration Expenses £100 Debit
- Sales £12,500 Credit
- Drawings £1,500 Debit (will go in the final income statement but not the 'trading' bit).

Once this has been done we can construct the trading account as shown in Table 5.1.

Table 5.1 Mike: Trading Income Statement

	£	£
Sales		12,500
Cost of Sales (see below*)		(5,000)
Gross Profit		7,500
Expenses		
Rent	3,500	
Loan Interest	100	
Administration Expenses	100	
		(3,700)
Net Profit		3,800

Cost of sales is what the cost to the company was for the goods that had been sold. The goods are hopefully sold at a higher price, and that price should also leave a surplus to cover the other expenses of the business. In the example in Table 5.1 it has been assumed that all of the goods purchased have been sold. In reality that will not be the case: companies hold stock (inventory). Therefore it will be necessary to do a stock take to see what has not been sold. Stock is valued at its cost price and not its resale value. Continuing this idea means that at the start of the period there will have been some stock brought forward from the previous period (unless the company has just started trading). So to ensure that we have got the correct figure for 'Cost of sales' we use the formula:

$$\text{Cost of sales} = \text{opening stock} + \text{purchases} - \text{closing stock}$$

Don't worry if this is the first time you have seen a statement like this (or that we haven't really discussed it). It is here to serve a purpose and we will come back to it in detail in a later chapter.

A brief insight into the balance sheet

Identifying the accounts, which feed into this statement, should be really easy. Look back at which ones weren't used to construct the income statement and you should find the following; cash, capital, bank loan, trade creditors, shop fittings, trade debtors and drawings. The only point of real note here is that the income statement and balance sheet work together using profit (or loss) so this will also need to be recorded somewhere.

In our example Mike's capital will consist of any cash that he introduced plus any profit that the business makes, minus any drawings. He introduced £7,000, made drawings of £1,500 while the business made a profit of £3,800. Consequently the owner's capital equals £9,300 (7,000 – 1,500 + 3,800). Understanding this allows us to construct the balance sheet shown in Table 5.2.

Table 5.2 Mike: Trading Balance Sheet

	£
Assets	
Non-current assets	
Property, plant and equipment	2,000
Current Assets	
Inventories	0
Trade receivables	1,000
Cash and cash equivalents	8,050
Total assets	11,050
Equity and Liabilities	
Equity	9,300
Non-current liabilities	1,000
Current liabilities	
Trade payables	750
Total equity and liabilities	11,050

Notice that in Table 5.2 the balance sheet balances. Again don't worry about this too much at this stage – we'll look at it later. However, the basic point behind all of this is to help with the preparation of the final statements. We can be confident with our trial balance and trading accounts at this stage as they balance.

SUMMARY

This chapter should have helped you understand why 'T' accounts are constructed in the first place and that each account should be periodically balanced off. All of the individual ledger accounts should be balanced off at the end of the accounting period, be it the end of a month, quarter or year. The debit and credit balances are then listed in two columns in a financial statement called the trial balance. Providing that the sum of the credit balance is the same as the sum of the debit balances we can make the assumption that the records are mathematically correct. However, it is still good practice to check your records against the limitations of the trial balance to ensure that there are no other errors. This trial balance, subject to some more alterations, such as cost of sales, mispostings, accruals and prepayments which we cover in the next chapter, will then be used as the basis for drawing up the balance sheet and income statement.

Remember a trial balance is your way of checking your bookkeeping skills as it helps to perform an arithmetic check. However, there are some notable drawbacks to the trial balance, which should prompt you to be vigilant when applying the double entry rule, and constructing 'T' accounts.

1   List the five circumstances in which a trial balance might balance even though some of the balances are incorrect.

■ _____

■ _____

■ _____

■ _____

■ _____

2   What is the purpose of the trial balance?
3   Indicate where each of the following items will be shown (in the trading income statement or balance sheet):

■   Trade Debtors
■   Cash and Bank
■   Bank Loans
■   Rent
■   Wages
■   Loan interest paid
■   Trade Creditors

4   Should the cost of equipment we have purchased be shown in the income statement?
5   What effect does profit have on capital?
6   A company takes out a loan to pay for a new van. Is the loan an asset?
7   A company has owned a van worth £10,000 for 2 years. It depreciates the van by £2,000 each year. What would be in the trial balance at the end of the second year for the van and its depreciation?
8   Does a trial balance list all the transactions made by the business?

1   Errors of omission and commission, compensating errors. Errors of principal and errors of original entry.
2   An arithmetic check to ensure that the double entry rule has been applied correctly. Debits should equal credits!
3   The answers are:

- Trade Debtors: balance sheet (current asset)
- Cash and Bank: balance sheet (current asset)
- Bank Loans: balance sheet (non-current liability)
- Rent: income statement (expense)
- Wages: income statement (expenses). If they are owed they would also be in the balance sheet (current liability)
- Loan interest paid: income statement (expense)
- Trade Creditors: balance sheet (current liability)

4   No! It will be shown in the balance sheet as a fixed asset.
5   Profit increases capital.
6   No: the van is an asset. The loan is a liability (it is money that is owed).
7   The values would be:

- Van (asset): £10,000. This is the cost of the van and would go on the balance sheet
- Depreciation (expense): £2,000. This is the depreciation charge for the second year and would be taken to the income statement.
- Provision for Depreciation: £4,000. This would go to the balance sheet and would allow the calculation of the net book value of the van (£6,000).

8   No: it lists a summary of the transactions, i.e. the balances on each account.

'T' ACCOUNTS FOR THE TRIAL BALANCE ACTIVITY

These are the answers to the Activity on p. 88. To help make this logical (if you got the activity wrong) you'll notice that there is a reference column included in the accounts. This represents the question number so that you can follow exactly what we have done.

Cash Account

Ref	DEBIT	Ref	CREDIT
1	7,000	2	3,500
4	1,000	5	2,000
6	10,000	8	4,250
9	1,500	10	100
		11	100
		12	1,500
		C/d	8,050
	19,500		19,500
B/d	8,050		

Capital Account

Ref	DEBIT	Ref	CREDIT
		1	7,000
C/d	7,000		
	7,000		7,000
		B/d	7,000

Rent Account

Ref	DEBIT	Ref	CREDIT
2	3,500		
		C/d	3,500
	3,500		3,500
B/d	3,500		

Purchases (Stock)

Ref	DEBIT	Ref	CREDIT
3	5,000		
		C/d	5,000
	5,000		5,000
B/d	5,000		

Trade Creditors Account

Ref	DEBIT	Ref	CREDIT
8	4,250	3	5,000
C/d	750		
	5,000		5,000
		B/d	750

Loan Account

Ref	DEBIT	Ref	CREDIT
		4	1,000
C/d	1,000		
	1,000		1,000
		B/d	1,000

96

Fixtures and Fittings Account

Ref	DEBIT	Ref	CREDIT
5	2,000		
		C/d	2,000
	2,000		2,000
B/d	2,000		

Sales Account

Ref	DEBIT	Ref	CREDIT
		6	10,000
C/d	12,500	7	2,500
	12,500		12,500
		B/d	12,500

Trade Debtors Account

Ref	DEBIT	Ref	CREDIT
7	2,500	9	1,500
		C/d	1,000
	2,500		2,500
B/d	1,000		

Interest Payable (Loan Interest)

Ref	DEBIT	Ref	CREDIT
10	100		
		C/d	100
	100		100
B/d	100		

Wages (Admin) Account

Ref	DEBIT	Ref	CREDIT
11	100		
		C/d	100
	100		100
B/d	100		

Drawings Account

Ref	DEBIT	Ref	CREDIT
12	1,500		
		C/d	1,500
	1,500		1,500
B/d	1,500		

CHAPTER SIX

FINAL ADJUSTMENTS FOR SPORT AND LEISURE

On completion of this chapter you will be able to:

- Make adjustments to the trial balance (cost of sales, mispostings, accruals and prepayments, and others).

INTRODUCTION

In this chapter we will bring together the knowledge that you have gained from the earlier chapters so that we can move towards compiling the financial statements. However, before you can progress to constructing a set of financial statements you need to go through one last stage. This will involve making certain adjustments so that your accounts conform to the accounting principles that we took you through in Chapter 2. These adjustments are commonly known as 'Trial Balance adjustments' because they make use of information that was not taken into account when preparing the trial balance and therefore cause it to be adjusted.

Throughout the previous three chapters you should have been asking yourselves questions such as what happens to transactions that occurred in this accounting period but we won't pay (or get paid for) until the next one? How do I deal with stock because when I make a sale the money is not all profit? What happens if I forget to record a transaction in the ledgers? The answer to these questions (and one or two more) will be explained in this chapter. We will examine cost of sales (you were introduced to this at the end of Chapter 5), mispostings, accruals and prepayments. These are the types of things that you will encounter when sorting through the books of organisations that you may work for.

The income statement and balance sheet cannot be prepared until all of the accounts have been balanced and a trial balance constructed (see Chapter 5 for details on this). For any business this can be a lengthy exercise so it is probably a good idea to do it periodically.

However, no matter how up to date the accounting entries are, there are always a number of transactions that come up at the very end of the financial period. Due to the lateness of some transactions, the trading income statement and balance sheet may have already been drawn up. Clearly there will be a need for some more adjustments to be made before the final statements are drawn up when we consider all of the accounting concepts outlined in Chapter 2 – can you remember what these were?

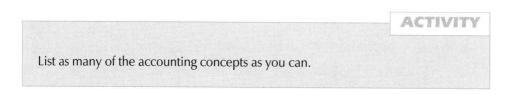

Hopefully you listed the following:

Going Concern, Accruals, Materiality, Business Entity, Money Measurement, Dual Aspect and Historical Cost, Prudence and Consistency.

If you have forgotten the meaning of any of these concepts we suggest that you have a quick flick through Chapter 2 again as they are fundamental underpinnings for what we are about to do. Once you are happy we can tackle the four key adjustments, cost of sales, mispostings, accruals and prepayments.

COST OF SALES

The income statement matches the cost of goods sold against sales income in order to calculate profit. We introduced you to this briefly in the last chapter. The purchases 'T' account allows us to record the costs of any goods that the business buys. However, in practice not all of the goods that the business buys will be sold by the end of the accounting period so purchases will not equal cost of sales. We need to take opening and closing stock into consideration to account for the difference. For example, if Kitlocker makes purchases in January of 100 pairs of swimming trunks at a stock cost of £10 each; sales are made of 75 of the units for £20, i.e. at a gross profit of £10 per unit, the accounting records for the business will show;

1   Purchases £1,000 (100 × £10)
2   Sales £1,500 (75 × £20)

In order for the income statement to accurately reflect this transaction we need to make an allowance for the 25 unsold pairs of swimming trucks, i.e. they must be removed from the cost of sales figure. This is easy when you apply the following formula (remember this from Chapter 5?):

$$\text{Cost of Sales} = \text{Opening stock} + \text{Purchases} - \text{Closing Stock}$$

For our example the cost of sales figure (assuming that the company started the year with no opening stock) will be:

Cost of Sales = £0 + £1000 – £250 (i.e. 25 pairs, worth £10 each)

Cost of Sales = £750

The cost of sales figure will then be put into the income statement under sales to help calculate gross profit as follows:

	£	£
Sales		1,500
Cost of Sales		750
Gross Profit		750

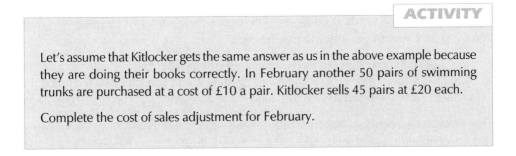

ACTIVITY

Let's assume that Kitlocker gets the same answer as us in the above example because they are doing their books correctly. In February another 50 pairs of swimming trunks are purchased at a cost of £10 a pair. Kitlocker sells 45 pairs at £20 each.

Complete the cost of sales adjustment for February.

Hopefully you worked it out like this.

$$\text{Cost of Sales} = \text{Opening Stock} + \text{Purchases} - \text{Closing Stock}$$

$$\text{Cost of Sales} = £250 \text{ (25 pairs left over from January)} + £500 \text{ (February Purchases)} - £250 \text{ (25 remaining pairs)}$$

Did you remember to include the opening stock?

There are a number of lessons that you should learn here about why the cost of sales adjustment is made. First, the cost of the units has been matched against the selling price of the units in accordance with the accruals concept. Any profit has only been recognised on the goods sold in accordance with the prudence concept. Closing stocks have been valued at cost, in our example £10 per pair of swimming trucks, because the potential profit of any unsold goods cannot be recognised until they are physically sold – this is again in accordance with the prudence concept.

There is, however, one more connection that you need to recognise: the value of closing stock (at the end of the period) will be used on the balance sheet.

MISPOSTINGS

Let's assume that you are preparing the accounts for your local 5-a-side football team and you have successfully balanced the trial balance. At first you will be pleased but then you will remember that the trial balance is not a perfect tool, as it does not show any transactions that you have missed out entirely (omissions) or if you have made entries on the correct sides of wrong accounts (mispostings), for example you purchases five new match balls and recorded them on the purchases account instead of the fixed asset (equipment) account. Remember that you are not going to sell the match balls – you are going to use them.

If and when this type of situation occurs you will need to do something about it. The trial balance has been constructed so we need to make our second type of adjustment – 'mispostings'. These are fairly straightforward to do as they follow the double entry rule. That is to say you will need to complete a debit and a credit entry to rectify your mistake. We'll continue with our example to illustrate this.

- Debit the equipment account (this will record your equipment)
- Credit Purchases (this cancels the earlier posting if you consider that recording an amount on this side will reduce the value of the account).

That should have been easy. Now have a go at drawing up the 'T' accounts for the following two activity questions and then make the necessary adjustments for misposting.

Construct the 'T' accounts for the following.

1   Your 5-a-side football team purchased some new goal nets for £100 cash and made the following *incorrect* entries:

   ▪ Debit Purchases £100
   ▪ Credit Cash and Bank

2   The telephone bill arrives for £50

   ▪ Debit Rent, Rates and Insurance
   ▪ Credit Trade Creditors

Now correct the entries.

You should have made these changes;

1   Debit Equipment £100
   Credit Purchases £100

2   Debit Telephone £50
   Credit Rent, Rates and Insurance £50.

ACCRUALS

You will have first come across the term 'accruals' in Chapter 2 as it is one of the most important accounting conventions that you need to understand. By now you should have a good understanding of the definition and when and how the concept is applied. Accruals will crop up in a sport and leisure setting, just as they do elsewhere. Because 'business life' is divided up into accounting periods we are faced with an immediate problem; which of the transactions should be included in the accounts for this year? This is due to the fact that the income statement and the balance sheet are drawn up for one year only but the business is a going concern and therefore 'lives' through many periods.

As you should know by now, profit is calculated by matching the income that has been earned during an accounting period with the expenses that have been incurred for that period. This is known as the accruals concept. Consequently, income and expenses should be attached to the accounting period that they relate to even though they may be paid in a different accounting period. The application of the accruals concept is therefore integral to constructing an income statement that offers a true and fair view.

A business will sometimes incur expenses before it has paid for them. A good example of this is electricity. Electricity bills are paid quarterly in arrears but when we are preparing the accounts for a period we need to show the expenses incurred for that period even if we have yet to be billed for them. How this would be dealt with is explained below.

If the electricity bill arrives and is paid for immediately the business will debit light and heat (+Expense) and Credit cash and bank (–Asset). If it isn't paid immediately then the business will deal with it slightly differently and will debit light and heat (+Expense) and credit trade creditors (+Creditors). These entries will be made during normal day-to-day activities, will be recorded in the appropriate 'T' accounts and will ultimately end up in the trial balance.

However, if at the end of an accounting period electricity has been used for which a bill has not yet been received, the expense must be 'accrued'. (You will need to estimate what you think you will be charged for the electricity for this period.) In this situation the business will debit light and heat (+Expense) and credit trade creditors (+Creditors) with the estimated amount. This will allow the business to recognise the expense as something that it owes when it moves into the next accounting period and will ensure that the expenses that have been incurred for the period have been charged in the income statement.

Accrued income can be dealt with in much the same way. If we assume that Kitlocker makes sales at the end of an accounting period on credit and does not send the invoice, it still needs to show on the income statement. Remember that the income statement must show the total income earned during the period. As such the following entries will be required: debit 'Trade debtors' (+Asset) and credit 'Sales' (+Income). Hopefully this will seem straightforward but you need to understand it as it is common for students to make errors here.

PREPAYMENTS

Prepayments are simply the opposite of accruals: prepayments are expenses that have been paid in advance (i.e. they do not relate to this accounting period). Prepayments are therefore a way for us to show amounts that are paid for expenses incurred in readiness for a future accounting period. An example of this is when you pay for the insurance on your car. Normally it will be paid in full at the start of the coming year. However, if you insurance was due for renewal in August and the accounting period ends in March you will have paid for 5/12ths of the insurance for the next accounting period. If we assume that the insurance cost £240 then only £140 relates to the current accounting period. This is the amount that will be included on the income statement with the remaining £100 being recorded in the trade debtor account as it represents five months' insurance cover that is owed to the business.

SUMMARY

The adjustments to the trial balance that you have been introduced to here represent those that you will be most likely to meet in your future careers. You must be aware that making such adjustments will alter the trial balance so that it offers a true and fair view of an organisation before the final accounts are drawn up. Consequently the information will now be ready for the preparation of the final set of financial statements. That is what we will do in the next chapter and then we will look at interpreting annual reports and using financial information. Putting the accounts together is easy – it is the ability to interpret financial statements that needs real skill!

QUESTIONS FOR REVIEW

1 Explain what is meant by (i) an accrued expense and (ii) a prepaid expense?
2 How do accruals and prepayments affect the trial balance?
3 A business paid its annual rent of £12,000 in August. The business has an accounting period that ends in March. Explain the accounting entries that would be needed for the rent.
4 What is Gross Profit and how is it calculated?
5 What is Net Profit?

1   (i) An accrued expense is an amount that is owed but has not yet been paid. For example, a company's telephone charges will be billed quarterly in arrears. If its year end is part way through a quarter it will estimate the phone charges that it thinks will have accrued and put that in the accounts.

    (ii) A prepaid expense is the opposite of the above, i.e. it has been paid in advance (for example car insurance).

2   They would be adjustments to the respective accounts (and would be shown on the balance sheet as prepayments and current liabilities).

3   Only the period August to March is in this accounting period. So only 8/12 of the payment is for this year so of the £12,000 paid, only £8,000 is for this year. The other £4,000 is a prepayment and will be charged as an expense in next year's accounts.

4   Gross profit is profit before deducting operating expenses, i.e. interest and tax. It is calculated as Gross Profit = Sales Revenue minus cost of sales.

5   Net Profit is Sales Revenue minus all expenses. It is calculated as Gross Profit minus all other expenses.

PART 3
THE MEANING

CHAPTER SEVEN

THE FINANCIAL STATEMENTS

On completion of this chapter you will be able to:

- Understand and explain the information needed to construct the financial statements.
- Understand the reporting and measurement of financial performance and position. Understand and explain the accounts of non-trading organisations.
- Explain the difference between cash and profit.

INTRODUCTION

By now you should be able to confidently construct and adjust a trial balance and be ready to move on to the final stage in constructing final accounts. In Chapters 1 and 6 you were given some brief information about the income statement and balance sheet, which was necessary to place what you were doing into context. The statements will now, finally, be considered in detail so that you can see what the accountant has to do in practice. Consequently, most of this chapter focuses the format of an income statement, balance sheet and cash flow statement.

As well as being of interest to management, the financial health of an organisation will be interesting to all of the external users of financial information that we examined in Chapter 1. We can use the income statement and balance sheet to examine this concept by measuring financial performance and financial position. The income statement can be used to work out how profitable an organisation has been over a given accounting period, therefore highlighting financial performance; and as the balance sheet summarises what the business owns and owes its can be used to show us financial position. However, while we examine all of this information we need to be aware of the importance of cash. Cash is different to profit and the cash flow statement needs to be used in conjunction with the income statement and balance sheet to show further details about the organisation and its performance.

You have seen the regulatory framework in action already so in addition to the three key statements outlined above, this chapter will begin to show you the real implications of it and start to make you aware of why you really need to know everything we have told you so far. Many general accounting books go into great detail about various systems and procedures, many of which you have not been subjected to so far because you are not training to be accountants. What you have been doing, though, is developing a general awareness of accounting practices and information so that you understand the final accounts.

The basics of what you will be doing in the sport and leisure industry may be based around much of the information so far. However, by virtue of your future qualifications you may become more and more involved in the detailed financial affairs of organisations through your personal involvement with sport clubs and teams, small leisure organisations and the voluntary sector. Therefore, we also need to show you what these 'non-trading organisations' do when it comes to finance.

We have picked a bad time to write this book! At the time of writing there is much debate and soul-searching by accountants in many organisations about the format they should use to publish their financial statements. Should it be the ones recommended in the Companies Act or those as recommended by the International Accounting Standards Board? The dilemma is caused by the accountants trying to choose the one that best portrays a 'true and fair view'. However, it should be remembered that it is only listed companies that have this dilemma, other organisations are free to choose whatever format they like (providing it also gives a true and fair view).

INTERNATIONAL ACCOUNTING STANDARD 1

International Accounting Standard (IAS) 1 says that the set of financial statements should include

- Income statement
- Balance sheet
- A statement of changes in equity
- Cash flow statement
- Notes giving a summary of the accounting policies used and other explanations.

The statement of changes in equity is beyond the scope of this book and consequently we will not cover it. However, we do need to examine everything else and although we won't get bogged down in telling you how to write statements summarising accounting policies we will give you some examples from actual accounts. The three major statements will now be covered.

THE INCOME STATEMENT (PROFIT AND LOSS ACCOUNT)
– MEASURING FINANCIAL PERFORMANCE

The purpose of an income statement is to show you a history of financial performance (profitability) of the business over the accounting period. It is by definition retrospective because it covers the last accounting period (normally the last year). Businesses exist (in most cases) to generate wealth, or profit, and it is this wealth or profit that most people will be interested in. If you think back to the Manchester United case study that you read in Chapter 2, you will probably remember that the profitability of the football club was the principal reason that Malcolm Glazer bought the club.

The measurement of profit first requires the business to calculate the total revenue generated in a particular period. Following this the business will need to calculate the total expenses relating to the accounting period. The income statement will then deduct the total expenses from the total revenues. The difference will represent either profit (if revenue exceeds expense) or loss (if expenditure exceeds revenue).

KEY TERMS

REVENUE

A measure of the inflow of assets to a business. Such assets could take the form of cash or amounts owed by debtors. Some more traditional forms of revenue will be generated by the sale of goods, fees for services, subscriptions and interest received.

EXPENSE

A measure of the outflow of assets from a business, which are incurred as a result of generating revenue. Some of the more common types of expenses could be: the cost of buying goods that are then sold (cost of sales), wages and salaries, rent and rates, insurance, telecommunications etc.

Before we see what the income statement will look like you need to take note of a few extra points and issues because just to confuse you even further, IAS 1 allows two methods of presentation for the income statement: by 'function' of the expenses or by the 'nature' of the expense. The standard allows organisations to choose the one 'which most fairly represents the elements of the enterprise's performance'. The standard recognises that analysts will want to be able to compare the performance of several organisations and therefore will want to ensure that they are comparing like with like. To ensure that the necessary information is available the standard states that information on the nature of expenses, including depreciation and staff costs should be disclosed.

IAS 'by function' format

Income statement for the year ended DD/MM/YYYY

	£m
Revenue	X
Cost of sales	(X)
Gross profit	X
Other operating income	X
Distribution costs	(X)
Administrative expenses	(X)
Profit from operations	X
Net interest cost	(X)
Profit before tax	X
Income tax expense	(X)
Net profit for period	X

The notes accompanying the statement would disclose the depreciation and staff costs included in the above figures. So that you can appreciate how all of this will actually work in practice have a look at Blacks Leisure Group's income statement in Figure 7.1.

You can see from Blacks' income statement that it conforms to the 'by function format' suggested by the IAS. The statement itself details the key points i.e. that operating profit is about £22m and that profit after tax is £14.5m. We can, however, get some more information on, for example, where the revenue came from by looking into the notes to the accounts. A selection of such information for Blacks is highlighted in Figure 7.2.

INTERPRETING THE INCOME STATEMENT

When the income statement is presented to its users (much like the Blacks example) it is often only the net profit that is examined. Granted this is the primary measure of performance, but you must recognise that it is not the only one. In Chapter 8 you will see how we can analyse the figures contained in the income statement and balance sheet but for the purposes of this chapter you need to see the value of the income statement when seen on its own.

In order to evaluate the performance of a business effectively you will need to find out how the net profit, or 'profit for the year attributable to equity holders of the parent' in our Blacks example, is derived. The best way to do this is to analyse the level and amount of sales, the nature and amount of expenses and profit in relation to sales. We'll do this for the Blacks example to help you to understand what we mean.

The sales figure for 2006 can be compared to that of 2005. This shows us that Blacks has been able to make more sales (£297,238,000 compared to £293,967,000). Additionally,

Consolidated Income Statement

for the year ended 28 February 2006

	Note	**Year ended** **28 Feburary 2006** **£'000**	Year ended 28 Feburary 2005 £'000
Revenue	2	**297,238**	293,967
Cost of sales		**(128,112)**	(137,041)
Gross profit		**169,926**	156,926
Other income	2	**1,861**	985
Distribution costs		**(137,517)**	(125,417)
Administrative expenses		**(11,106)**	(11,534)
Operating profit	4	**22,364**	20,960
Finance costs	6	**(1,741)**	(1,021)
Finance income	6	**812**	459
Profit before tax		**21,435**	20,398
Tax expense	7	**(6,897)**	(6,612)
Profit for the year attributable to equity holders of the parent		**14,538**	13,786
Earnings per share (pence)	8		
– Basic		**34.57**	32.87
– Diluted		**33.88**	32.62

All amounts relate to continuing activities.

Figure 7.1 Blacks Leisure Group Income Statement

Source: From Blacks Leisure Group Plc
Annual Report and Financial Statements 2006.

Notes to the Financial Statements

for the year ended 28 February 2006

2. Revenue and other operating income

	2006 **£'000**	2005 £'000
Revenue from sale of goods	**297,238**	293,967
Other operating income	**1,861**	985

Other operating income consists of sub-let property income amounting to £1,226.000 (2005: £985,000) and other property related income of £635,000 (2005: £nil).

Figure 7.2 Blacks Leisure Group Notes to the Accounts

Source: From Blacks Leisure Group Plc
Annual Report and Financial Statements 2006.

in generating this revenue the company has managed to lower its cost of sales from £137,041,000 in the year ending February 2005 to £128,112,000 in the year ending February 2006. This suggests that its profitability is likely to improve.

Next we can examine the gross profit figure as both an absolute number and in relation to revenue. In absolute terms Blacks has a higher gross profit in 2006 than it did in 2005 (£169,126,000 compared with £159,926,000). Relative to revenue this is about 58 per cent in 2006 and 53 per cent in 2005 (so again higher in 2006). We will explain the reasoning and mechanics of this calculation in Chapter 8, however, it tells us basically that in 2006 for every £1 of revenue 58 pence is gross profit and in 2005 it was 53 pence.

The expenses of the business show us that distribution costs have increased from 2005 to 2006 and that administration costs have gone down slightly. You should note here that we would expect distribution costs to increase because Blacks has generated more in the way of sales revenue. Finally, net profit can be examined in the same way as gross profit. In absolute terms it has increased by £752,000 from 2005 to 2006 (£14,538,000 – £13,786,000), however, in relative terms it has remained the same at 5 per cent each year.

By using this basic analysis and the notes to the accounts (a section of which was illustrated in Figure 7.2) we can begin to build up a fuller picture of the financial performance of the organisations. The basic lesson in the Blacks example (without going through all of the notes) is that the company is performing quite well. Overall the organisation's gross profitability has increased from 2005 in line with an increase in revenue from the sale of goods although net profitability has remained the same. Before we move on to look at the balance sheet and cash flow statement you need to remember one more thing. The income statement recognises transactions for the period concerned irrespective of when cash changes hands and therefore shows the profit or loss achieved over an accounting period.

THE BALANCE SHEET: A SNAPSHOT OF THE FINANCIAL POSITION

The balance sheet is the financial statement that reflects the accounting equation – remember what this is? We covered this in detail in Chapter 3. The accounting equation states that the assets of the business will equal the capital and other liabilities (Assets = Capital + Liabilities). The equation, like the balance sheet, must balance. If you think back to when you studied maths at school you will realise that the equation can be rearranged so that Assets – Liabilities = Capital. This equation will help us to recognise the financial position of a business at a given point in time with the help of the balance sheet. We'll come back to this in a minute.

If we agree that the balance sheet reflects the accounting equation then we also agree that the balance sheet shows the financial position of the business because it shows us details of what the business owns and what it owes. It is often referred to as a 'snapshot' or 'picture' as it only shows us what is going on at a specific point in time. Normally the business will prepare its balance sheet at the close of business on the last day of the accounting period. In doing this, however, it has a weakness. A photograph only illustrates a specific moment and cannot show us what has happened before or after. It is the same for the balance sheet and as such it may not represent a typical trading position but we won't worry about this for the time being.

The balance sheet should distinguish between non-current assets and current assets. When classifying the assets you need to recognise the guidance provided by IAS 1. The standard states that current assets are:

- part of the organisation's operations;
- held for trading purposes;
- cash and cash equivalents.

All other assets will be classified as 'non-current' assets.

Similarly, the liabilities need to be split between 'current' and 'non-current'. Current liabilities are:

- within the normal course of business;
- due to be paid in the next financial year.

All other liabilities will be shown as 'non-current', see balance sheet on page 116.

Again the basic structure is all very well, but it is always more useful for your learning to see this in practice so let's have a look at what the Blacks Leisure Group's balance sheet looked like when its financial statements were constructed at its year end (Figure 7.3).

As was the case with Blacks' income statement, the balance sheet conforms to the guidelines of the IAS. The statement itself details the key issues that arise, such as the value of the organisation's total assets, total liabilities and total capital (looks like the information required for the accounting equation to us!). You will also notice that there are many references to 'notes to the accounts' here. As each individual business transaction will have been recorded in the organisation's ledger accounts a summary is given in the published balance sheet. The additional detail will be held like it was for the income statement. Have a quick look at Figure 7.4 so that you can see what we mean.

INTERPRETING THE BALANCE SHEET

Despite the fact that the balance sheet only illustrates a business's financial position at a given point in time, it does contain some quite useful information. As with the income statement, we will cover a deeper analysis in Chapter 8, but for now we can see what the balance sheet can tell us in its own right. The balance sheet can provide us with some useful information and insights into the financing and investing activities of a business.

Balance sheet as at DD/MM/YYYY

	£m	£m
Assets		
Non-current assets		
Property, plant and equipment	X	
Goodwill	X	
Other intangible assets	X̲	
		X
Current Assets		
Inventories	X	
Trade and other receivables	X	
Other current assets	X	
Cash and cash equivalents	X̲	
		X̲
Total assets		X̲
Equity and Liabilities		
Equity		
Issued capital	X	
Reserves	X	
Accumulated profits	X̲	
		X
Non-current liabilities		
Long-term borrowings	X	
Long-term provisions	X̲	
		X
Current Liabilities		
Trade and other payables	X	
Short-term borrowings	X	
Proposed dividends	X	
Tax payable	X̲	
		X̲
Total equity and liabilities		X̲

Consolidated Balance Sheet
for the year ended 28 February 2006

	Note	2006 £'000	2005 £'000
ASSETS			
Non-current assets			
Property, plant and equipment	10	**40,452**	33,832
Goodwill	11	**36,352**	36,352
Other intangible assets	12	**666**	–
Total non-current assets		**77,470**	70,184
Current assets			
Inventories	14	**54,350**	46,483
Trade and other receiveables	15	**14,074**	15,202
Derivative financial instruments	29	**711**	–
Cash and cash equivalents	16	**16,733**	12,021
Total current assets		**85,868**	73,706
TOTAL ASSETS		**163,338**	143,890
EQUITY AND LIABILITIES			
Equity and attributable to equity holders of the parent			
Share capital	17	**21,234**	21,850
Share premium	18	**23,910**	22,780
Reserve for own shares	19	**(401)**	(217)
Hedging reserve	20	**498**	–
Share-based payment reserve	20	**375**	135
Retained earnings	20	**63,964**	53,775
TOTAL EQUITY			
		109,580	98,323
Non-current liabilities			
Preference shares	17	**891**	–
Accruals and deferred income		**1,883**	1,117
Obligations under finance leases	22	**3,805**	24
Deferred tax liabilities	7	**74**	191
Long-term provisions	24	**161**	415
Total non-current liabilities		**6,814**	1,747
Current liabilities			
Trade and other payables	23	**39,346**	39,102
Current tax liabilities		**3,318**	3,442
Bank overdrafts	21	**3,025**	846
Obligations under leases	22	**674**	23
Short-term provisions	24	**581**	407
Total current liabilities		**46,944**	43,820
TOTAL LIABILITIES		**53,758**	45,567
TOTAL EQUITY AND LIABILITIES		**163,338**	143,890

Figure 7.3 Blacks Leisure Group Balance Sheet

Source: From Blacks Leisure Group Plc
Annual Report and Financial Statements 2006.

Notes to the Financial Statements

for the year ended 28 February 2006

14 Inventories

	2006 £'000	2005 £'000
Finished goods	54,350	43,483

During the year £3,224,000 (2005: £3,090,000) of inventory write-downs were expensed within cost of sales.

15 Trade and other receivables

	2006 £'000	2005 £'000
Trade receivables	6,535	7,879
Other debtors	1,767	1,608
Prepayments and accrued income	5,772	5,715
	14,074	15,202

Trade and other receivables are non-interest bearing and are generally on 28-day terms.

The Directors consider that the carrying amount of these assets are approximate to their fair value.

16 Cash and cash equivalents

	2006 £'000	2005 £'000
Cash at bank and in hand	6,548	12,021
Short-term deposits	10,185	–
	16,733	12,021

Cash at bank and in hand earns interest at floating rates based on daily bank deposit rates. Short-term deposits are made for varying periods of between one day and one month depending on the immediate cash requirements of the Group, and earn interest at the respective short-term deposit rates. The fair value of cash and cash equivalents are considered to be their book value.

For the purposes of the consolidated cash flow statement, cash and cash equivalents comprise the following:

	2006 £'000	2005 £'000
Cash at bank and in hand	6,548	12,021
Short-term deposits	10,185	–
Bank overdrafts (note 21)	(3,025)	(846)
16,733	13,708	11,175

At 28 February 2006, the Group had available £22,900,000 (2005: £21,900,00) of undrawn committed borrowing facilities in respect of which all conditions precedent had been met. The number of months until expiration of the facility is five at the year-end. Subsequent to the year-end the facility has been renewed for a further two years, further details of which are provided on page 11.

Figure 7.4 Blacks Leisure Group Notes to the Accounts 2

Source: From Blacks Leisure Group Plc
Annual Report and Financial Statements 2006.

We can, for example, see how much cash the organisation has that it could use, if required, to pay its creditors or purchase new assets. In 2006 Blacks has £16,733,000 in cash compared to £12,021,000 in 2005. This will give the organisation some flexibility when it comes to paying its debts.

Next we could examine the mix of business assets. The relationship between fixed and current assets is quite important because businesses with too few current assets could get into financial difficulty if creditors called in their debts. There is not a 'golden rule' about the correct mix of fixed and current assets. There are many factors that will impact on that structure: the type of organisation and how the company is financed are two major ones. If the company has loans, it will need to pay the interest – remember the Leeds United case study in Chapter 1? Blacks has a fairly equal split between fixed and current assets in 2006 (£77,470,000 fixed assets compared to £85,868,000 current assets). This asset mix indicates that the organisation could convert about 50 per cent of the business's value quite easily and could therefore cope if a significant number of its creditors asked it to settle its debts.

Heavy borrowing brings with it a commitment to high interest charges and large capital repayments at regular intervals that are legally enforced. Finances raised from the owners of the business will not have the same obligations: there is not a contractual obligation to pay dividends to shareholders. The owners of a business receive their 'rewards' from the residue of profit after all other obligations have been met. For Blacks there is no real problem as its current assets cover its current liabilities.

RELATIONSHIP BETWEEN THE INCOME STATEMENT AND BALANCE SHEET

The income statement and balance sheet should not be seen in isolation or as substitutes for one another. Instead you should use them in tandem so that you can build up a stronger idea of an organisation's financial health. You should hopefully have noticed when looking at all of the income statement and balance sheet examples in this book that the two statements are actually interlinked. The income statement can be seen as linking the balance sheet at the beginning of an accounting period with the balance sheet at the end of the accounting period.

When a business starts at the beginning of a financial period a balance sheet can be drawn up to reflect the opening position, i.e. how many assets it owns, how many creditors it owes and how much it is worth (capital). After an appropriate amount of time has passed an income statement can be constructed to illustrate how much profit or loss has been incurred during that time. A new balance sheet will then be derived to reflect the new financial position at the end of the accounting period and from this we can see how well the business has done!

CASH FLOW STATEMENT

Since being in business is about money, information about cash will be very important. Without sufficient cash a person or organisation will get into financial difficulty (just ask Leeds United) or in some cases be declared bankrupt. With this in mind, although the income statement is vital in helping to discover the profitability of a business it does not give us a clear insight into any problems the business may have with its cash flow. Do you know why? If not, think back to Chapter 2 and the accruals concept.

ACCRUALS

The accruals basis of accounting requires the non-cash effects of transactions and other events to be reflected in the financial statements for the accounting period in which they occur and not in the period when the cash is paid or received. For example, if a sale is agreed in 2006 but the terms of the deal are that the cash is not received until 2007, the transaction should be shown in the accounts for 2006.

Because we base all of our double entry bookkeeping on the accruals concept any cash problems that a business may have can be disguised. Any items of large expenditure will not have an immediate impact on the income statement but will have a significant impact on the amount of cash that a business has available to it. If you think about this logically it is rather simple – a business needs cash so that it can operate!

Remember what we said at the end of the income statement section. The income statement recognises transactions when they occur, regardless of when cash changes hands and therefore shows the profit or loss achieved over an accounting period – so why all the fuss? Well it is because in business people and organisations will not normally accept anything other than cash in settlement of activity. A business will have to pay its employees in cash, its suppliers in cash and its customers will have to pay in cash. Consequently if the business does not have enough cash it will probably fail – after all you can't pay people with profit. This means that when you examine and construct financial statements you need to understand cash flow so that you can appreciate how the business will continue to survive or take advantage of new opportunities.

In 1991, the financial reporting standards people realised this and wrote FRS 1. Because the income statement (or P&L as it was then) and balance sheet were based on accruals and not liquidity, the concept of going concern was compromised. As a result FRS 1 requires all apart from the very smallest companies to produce and publish a cash flow forecast in their annual reports.

The cash flow statement is basically a financial summary of all of the cash receipts and payments over an accounting period. All of the payments of a particular type are grouped together to give one figure; for example, all cash payments to creditors will be totalled up and the single figure recorded. Following this the total payments will be deducted from the total receipts to give a net increase or decrease in cash over the period. We'll have a look at the cash flow statement for the Blacks Leisure Group so that you can see this in practice in just a minute.

Since 1991 the IAS has emerged and IAS 1 refers readers to IAS 7 for details of the required presentation needed for the cash flow statement. The statement should separate cash flows into operating, investing and financing activities to show the changes during the year to cash and cash equivalents.

The classifications are defined as:

Operating: these are the main revenue producing activities of the organisation that are not investing or financing activities. They will include cash received from customers and cash paid to suppliers and employees.

Investing: these activities are the acquisition and disposal of long-term assets and other investments that are not considered to be cash equivalents.

Financing: these activities result in changes to the size and composition of the equity and borrowings.

Hopefully you will have remembered from the earlier chapters, and the previous few paragraphs, that profit and cash are not the same thing. Therefore it is important that the readers of the statements (many of whom will not be financially literate) can readily distinguish between them. The cash flow statement will do this and will also show immediately how much cash the organisation has (i.e. the 'liquidity' of the business), and how much cash is generated by the operating side of the business (as opposed to other activities).

IAS 7 encourages organisations to use the following format:

	£m
Cash flows from Operating Activities	
Cash receipts from customers	X
Cash paid to suppliers	(X)
Cash paid to employees	(X)
Cash paid for other operating expenses	(X)
Cash generated from operations	X
Interest paid	(X)
Income taxes paid	(X)
Net cash flow from operating activities	**X**

Cash flows from Investing Activities

Purchase of non-current assets	**(X)**
Proceeds of sales of non-current assets	X
Net cash used in investing activities	**X**

Cash flows from Financing Activities

Proceeds from issue of share capital	X
Proceeds from long-term borrowing	X
Dividend paid	(X)
Net cash used in financing activities	**X**

Net increase in cash and cash equivalents A+B+C	X
Cash and cash equivalents at start of period	X
Cash and cash equivalents at end of period	X

Note: The three statements are interrelated. For example, consider the impact on the statements if an organisation sold a delivery van for £4,000 that it bought for £15,000 and had used for three years and had charged £9,000 depreciation against it during that period to the accounts.

The income statement (and notes) would show that there had been a loss of £2,000 on the disposal of a non-current asset (proceeds £4,000, initial cost of £15,000 and depreciated by £9,000). The balance sheet (and notes) would show the adjustment to net book value of the non-current assets caused by the disposal of the van (i.e. a reduction of £6,000). The cash flow statement in the 'Cash flows from Investing Activities' section would show an income of £4,000. Have a look at Figure 7.5 and see what the Blacks Leisure Group cash flow statement looks like.

Once again the Blacks example clearly puts the IAS regulation into practice. The cash flow statement tells us how well the business has generated cash during the accounting period and, importantly, where that cash has gone. Net cash flow for the Blacks Leisure Group is strong and resulted in an increase of £2,533,000 in 2006, however this was less than during the same period in 2005 (£5,235,000). New business assets absorbed quite a substantial amount of cash in 2006 (almost £10m) and the taxman has also taken his fair share. Overall, the net cash flow figure is healthy and the business has room to spend during the next financial period.

Because the income statement only shows us details of financial performance, and therefore business wealth, it is useful to have an additional statement that highlights cash flows resulting from trading activities. Because cash flows are needed as one of the main financial statements it is important that you understand both how to construct them and how the statement interacts with the income statement and balance sheet.

Consolidated Cash Flow Statement

for the year ended 28 February 2006

	Note	Year ended 28 Feburary 2006 £'000	Year ended 28 Feburary 2005 £'000
Cash generated from operations	31	24,385	25,900
Interest paid		(1,625)	(1,010)
Tax paid		(7,151)	(6,257)
Net cash from operating activities		15,609	18,633
Cash flows from investing activities			
Purchase of property, plant and equipment		(9,893)	(12,392)
Purchase of intangible assets		(666)	–
(Payments)/proceeds from disposal of property, plant and equipment		(64)	1,129
Interest received		812	459
Net cash used in investing activities		(9,901)	((10,804)
Cash flows from investing activities			
Proceeds from issue of share capital		1,405	434
Purchase of own shares		(184)	(189)
Sale of own shares		–	263
Dividends paid	9	(4,349)	(3,596)
Payment of finance lease liabilities		(47)	(56)
Capital receipts		–	550
Net cash used in financing activities		(3,175)	(2,594)
Net increase in cash and cash equivalents		2,533	5,235
Cash and cash equivalents at the beginning of the year		11,175	5,940
Cash and cash equivalents at the end of the year	16	13,708	11,175

Figure 7.5 Blacks Leisure Group Cash Flow Statement

Source: From Blacks Leisure Group Plc
Annual Report and Financial Statements 2006.

NON-TRADING ORGANISATIONS

The previous sections on the income statement, balance sheet and cash flow statement focus on the requirements for organisations of a significant size and status. However, as we have tried to emphasise throughout this book, you are more likely to come into contact with the financial statements of smaller organisations on a more regular basis. With this in mind it is useful for you to see how things will differ for non-trading organisations.

The objectives of non-trading and not-for-profit organisations are to provide services to their members; not to generate profits. Although the financial statements of non-trading and not-for-profit organisations are not covered by the regulations of the Companies Act and the International Accounting Standards Board they will still be prepared using the same principles. Some small clubs and societies may just keep a record of receipts and payments. However, this would not be very informative and consequently the majority of clubs (especially those with assets), irrespective of their size, will prepare an income statement and a balance sheet.

There may be differences in the objectives of the clubs and societies from those of profit-seeking companies but the fundamental accounting will still be the same. Consequently, you should have no trouble in adapting your knowledge of accounting to be able to work in this type of organisation. The language may change: profits and losses become surpluses and deficits, capital becomes the accumulated funds, but the principles are exactly the same.

A swimming club may have several sources of income: subscriptions, sale of kit and fund raising activities (for example a Valentine's Day Dinner and Dance). The income state-ment would show the net surplus from each one of the activities with separate records being kept to record further details of each sphere of activity. For example, the 'sale of kit' records would show a trading account and balance sheet for that operation but only the resulting surplus would be shown in the club's income statement. Similarly, the Dinner and Dance records would show details of income from ticket sales and the expenses of organising the event and all related transactions but only the surplus would be shown on the income statement. Any assets (kit yet to be sold, Romeos yet to pay for their tickets) and liabilities (unpaid suppliers for the kit and the fee for the thrash metal band that played at the dance) would be shown in the club's balance sheet.

If you grasped the key issues out of this then it will be useful for you to see what the financial statement of non-trading organisations looks like. Let's see how the financial statements prepared by the British Triathlon Association (BTA) (Figures 7.6 and 7.7) differ from those of the Blacks Leisure Group shown earlier in this chapter.

Hopefully you can see how the two sets of financial statements are similar in their standard layout; the notable difference being the amount of information included. This is indicative of what the accounts of non-trading organisations will look like. Generally speaking the accounts are much easier to understand and should give you the confidence to prepare something similar should you need to.

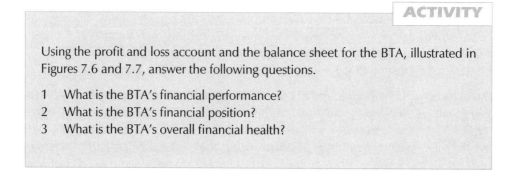

ACTIVITY

Using the profit and loss account and the balance sheet for the BTA, illustrated in Figures 7.6 and 7.7, answer the following questions.

1 What is the BTA's financial performance?
2 What is the BTA's financial position?
3 What is the BTA's overall financial health?

THE BRITISH TRIATHLON ASSOCIATION LIMITED

PROFIT AND LOSS ACCOUNT

FOR THE YEAR ENDED 31 MARCH 2006

	Notes	2006 £	2005 £
Income	2	2,338,163	2,198,773
Administrative Costs		(2,328,561)	(2,196.359)
Operating Profit/(Loss)	3	9,602	2,414
Interest Receivable		5,180	2,238
Profit/(Loss) on ordinary activities before taxation		14,782	4,652
Taxation	5	–	–
Profit/(Loss) on ordinary activities after taxation		14,782	4,652
Retained profit brought forward		19,001	14,349
Retained profit carried forward	11	33,783	19,001

Figure 7.6 British Triathlon Association Profit and Loss Account

Source: From the British Triathlon Association Limited Directors' Report and Accounts for the year ended March 2006.

Overall the BTA's financial performance is good, given that the organisation is there to provide a service and not make substantial profits. The income figures show us that the BTA has generated more income (£2,338,163 in 2006 compared to £2,198,773 in 2005). Additionally, in generating this income it also increased its administrative costs from £2,196,359 in 2005 to £2,328,561 in 2006. The gross profit figure (in this case operating profit) in absolute terms is higher in 2006 than in 2005 (£9,602 compared with £2,414). There is little point in examining the relationship between operating profit and income, as it will be insignificant. Finally, the retained profit carried forward figures, in absolute terms, demonstrate that the BTA is doing quite well. It has increased by £14,782 from 2005 to 2006 (£33,783 – £19,001).

In terms of financial position the BTA is well balanced. There is plenty of cash in the organisation's account (£282,700 in 2006) and total current assets can just about cover all of the organisation's creditors falling due within one year (£678,600 compared to £660,326). The mixture of fixed and current assets is very good as the BTA has only

THE BRITISH TRIATHLON ASSOCIATION LIMITED

BALANCE SHEET

AS AT 31 MARCH 2006

	Notes	2006 £	2006 £	2005 £	2005 £
Tangible fixed assets	6		50,969		40,470
Current assets					
Stock	7	183,831		39,580	
Debtors	8	212,069		226,267	
Cash at bank and in hand		282,700		64,718	
		678,600		330,565	
Creditors					
Amounts falling due within one year	9	660,326		316,574	
Net current assets			18,274		13,991
Total assets less current liabilities			69,243		54,461
Net Assets			69,243		54,461
RESERVES					
Members Special Reserve	10		35,460		35,460
Profit and loss account	11		33,783		19,001
MEMBERS FUNDS			69,243		54,461

These financial statements have been prepared in accordance with the special provisions relating to small companies within Part VII of the Companies Act 1985 and the Financial Reporting Standard for Smaller Entities (effective January 2005).

Figure 7.7 British Triathlon Association Balance Sheet

Source: From the British Triathlon Association Limited Directors' Report and Accounts for the year ended March 2006.

£50,969 tied up in tangible fixed assets in 2006. If the creditors called in their debts the BTA could probably convert its £678,600 current assets into cash to pay them relatively quickly. The organisation has no long-term liabilities and therefore is supported solely by its member's funds. This is a great position to be in as it allows the board of directors to control the organisation easily and without external pressures from creditors.

In summary, the financial health of the BTA is good. The organisation is not stretching itself and has sufficient funds to cover all of its responsibilities. Hopefully your answers were similar to ours. If not can you see where we are coming from and more importantly do you agree? Remember that organisations such as the BTA are quite easy to manage financially as they are based on member's subscriptions. This means that they can only use the money they have for the day-to-day running of the business and do not have the financial pressures of other trading companies.

SUMMARY

This chapter has taken you on a fairly long journey through the meaning, preparation and publication of the three main financial statements so that you can be confident when reading them. You have seen the impact of the regulatory framework in practice through the examples drawn from the Blacks Leisure Group and the British Triathlon Association. These examples have demonstrated how sport and leisure organisations, no matter what their size and sector, conform to the standards set out by the IAS.

The three statements work in unison to develop a picture of the financial health of an organisation. The income statement specifically can be used to measure financial performance or profitability, while the balance sheet is used to examine an organisation's financial position. However, the impact of each of the three statements is important to understand; in isolation they are not as useful.

You performed some basic analysis on the income statement and balance sheet, which should have highlighted their usefulness – the statements are worth much more than just the figures that are shown. Furthermore, to obtain valuable detail you need to delve deeper into an annual report and examine the notes. These notes explain how certain figures are calculated and under which accounting conventions they are derived. The next chapter will take this analysis much further and show how we can really make some good use out of an annual report.

ADDITIONAL CASE STUDY

Why not go back to the Arena Leisure case study that we asked you to look at in Chapter 1 and conduct the same analysis as we have done for Blacks Leisure Group? If you haven't already done so get on-line and download its annual report. It can be found at www.arenaleisureplc.com.

QUESTIONS FOR REVIEW

1   What does the income statement report?
2   What does the balance sheet show?
3   Are cash and profit the same thing?

1   The income statement reports the operating results of the organisation for the year. It shows, in financial terms, the activities of the organisation.

2   The balance sheet is a statement of the organisation's assets and liabilities. However, it is only a 'snapshot': it shows the situation at the time it was compiled. As soon as there is a transaction, it will change!

3   No, no and no. No way! NO! The answer is NO! Cash is cash: it is real, you can see it, you can spend it and you can touch it. Profit is not real: it is the 'residue' that remains after all expenses for a period have been deducted from incomes for a period. Note the answer says 'for a period' and not 'in a period'. This is because of the accruals concept.

CHAPTER EIGHT

INTERPRETING ANNUAL REPORTS

On completion of this chapter you will be able to:

- Explain the purpose of analysing financial statements.
- Appraise an organisation's financial position and performance through the application of ratio analysis and interpretation of the Annual Report.

INTRODUCTION

So far your studies through most of this book have focused on the preparation of accounts. However, as we have told you all along, our purpose is not to teach you how to become an accountant but to give you the knowledge, understanding and confidence to read a set of financial reports and to talk to and understand an accountant. Chapter 7 has illustrated how all of the stages in the accounting process are managed and ultimately why the major statements are constructed – and even demonstrated how you could basically analyse the main financial statements. However, constructing accurate financial statements, although a brilliant skill in its own right, is only half the story. The real purpose of this book is to show you, and to help you understand, what it all means. What does it really mean if company has a gross profit of £10m? What else do you need to know? What are the financial strengths and weaknesses of a business? How does one organisation compare to another in the same industry? The way that we can answer these questions, and as ever many more, is by starting to dissect annual reports.

In this chapter we are going to show you how different financial ratios help in analysing and interpreting financial information and ultimately give you the skills to evaluate the performance, position, solvency and efficiency of a business. This will help you to assess how well a company is performing and adds to the basic analysis that you undertook on the profit and loss account of the British Triathlon Association at the end of Chapter 7. We'll show you how all of this works by applying 'theory' to JJB Sports plc. This will give you a tangible example to work with and come back to when you have to do your own ratio analysis in the future.

DISSECTING ANNUAL REPORTS

Before any calculations are made you will be pleased to know that some of the first things that you should look for when working out how well a company is doing will be found at the very beginning of an annual report. Normally an annual report will contain at least three key bits of information that you can use. These are the accounts, the key reports (Chairman, Chief Executive and Directors), the auditor's report and any other important information. Therefore, the key reports are a great place to start. They will give you information about general performance, the major events that have taken place across the year, changes to the organisation in terms of staffing, accounting practice, exceptional items etc. and the wider industry situation – this will help you place everything into context. For example, when ITV Digital collapsed most of the Football League teams will have shown a drop in revenue and potential poor annual accounts. We therefore have a good reason to explain the situation.

It is important that you begin to see how all of this works in practice. As we mentioned in the introduction this chapter is based on the annual report of JJB Sports plc. This is therefore a good place to introduce you to the organisation and explain in general terms its annual report findings.

CASE STUDY

DISSECTING ANNUAL REPORTS – JJB SPORTS PLC

JJB Sports plc is the UK's leading quoted sports retailer whose main aims are to supply high quality, branded sports and leisure clothing, footwear and accessories at competitive prices and to expand on its portfolio of successful health clubs. The company started in 1971 by acquiring a single sports store. However, by 1994 its portfolio had grown to 120 stores, at which point the company was floated on the London Stock Exchange. At present JJB trades from over 430 stores across the UK and has a chain of combined health club/superstores.

In the accounting period to 29 January 2006 the company saw a disappointing fall in profits. The industry is in a state of change with more competition squeezing prices. For JJB the industry problem is manifested on two fronts: its retail business and its health clubs. To address the additional competition JJB has become more aggressive with its pricing strategy but this has had an obvious impact on profit margins.

interpreting annual reports

The company has agreements with major English Premier League Football Clubs and the English National Football team and is looking to the availability of new replica kits and on-the-field success to help improve its financial performance over the next accounting periods. Coupled with some developments in the health club business, JJB hopes that its long-term strategies will help it come out of its current problems. We began to analyse JJB's annual report in the introduction to this case study but to further understand what is going on a review of JJB's operating results can be found in Figure 8.1.

JJB Chief Executive's statement

Serious About Value

Review of operating results

The operating results for the 52 weeks to 29 January 2006 and those for the 53 weeks to 30 January 2005, are shown below.

	Revenue		Operating profit (1) before HO/DC allocation		Operating profit (1) after HO/DC allocation	
	2006	2005 Restated	**2006**	2005 Restated	**2006**	2005 Restated
	£'000	£'000	**£'000**	£'000	**£'000**	£'000
Stand-alone retail stores	**656,086**	710,647	**71,705**	103,376	**23,241**	55,254
Leisure Division (including associated retail stores)	**89,152**	62,692	**15,071**	9,639	**11,108**	6,852
	745,238	773,339	**86,776**	113,015	**34,349**	62,106
Head office and distribution centre costs (HO/DC)			**(52,427)**	(50,909)		
Operating profit (1)			**34,349**	62,106	**34,349**	62,106

(1) Operating profit is stated after crediting net exceptional operating items of £1,035,000 (2005: restated – charging £835,000) which are detailed in the Consolidated income statement on page 36.

Total revenue for the 52 weeks to 29 January 2006 is 3.6 per cent lower than for the 53 weeks to 30 January 2005 (2.4 per cent lower on a 52 week comparison). The decrease in like-for-like revenue of locations which have traded for over 52 weeks, on a 52 week comparison bais, is 4.3 per cent.

Figure 8.1 JJB Sports Operating Results

Source: From JJB Sports plc Annual Report and Financial Statements 2005–2006.

The review of operating results highlights the market problems that the case study introduction suggested. The stand-alone retail stores generate a significant amount of revenue to the business but between 2005 and 2006 there has been a reduction in sales of around £54.5m (£710,647,000 – £656,086,000). Additionally, the Head Office and distribution centre costs have increased and this has also led to lower operating profits.

It is also useful at this point to consider some of the analysis that was covered in Chapter 7, namely, how we can interpret the basics of the income statement and balance sheet (these are shown in Figures 8.2 and 8.3). In terms of financial performance JJB is doing all right, although its overall profitability has reduced from around £45m in 2005 to around £30m in 2006. Its financial position is also all right. It has an even split between fixed and current assets and does not have a significant amount of long-term credit because the company is owned by lots of different shareholders. JJB is therefore financially healthy albeit not as well as it was last year!

JJB Sports plc

Consolidated income statement
For the 52 weeks to 29 January 2006

	Note	52 weeks to 29 January 2006 £'000	53 weeks to 30 January 2005 Restated £'000
Continuing operations			
Revenue	3	**745,238**	773,339
Cost of sales		**(393,075)**	(402,082)
Gross profit		**352,163**	371,257
Other operating income	3	**3,177**	3,079
Distribution expenses		**(21,722)**	(19,272)
Administration expenses		**(30,705)**	(31,637)
Selling expenses		**(268,564)**	(261,321)
Operating profit		**34,349**	62,106
Operating profit is stated after (charging) crediting			
Creation of provision relating to legal penalty	25	**(1882)**	(2,000)
Release of legal cost accrual		**–**	2,000
Net gain (loss) on disposal of property, plant and equipment		**2,917**	(835)
		1,035	(835)
Finance income	8	**8,896**	9,036
Finance costs	9	**(9,498)**	(8,692)
Profit before taxation	6	**33,747**	62,450
Taxation	10	**(3,510)**	(17,287)
Profit after taxation for the period attributable to equity holders of the parent	33	**30,237**	45,163
Basic earnings per share Pence	13	**13.10**	19.54
Diluted earnings per share Pence	13	**13.10**	19.51

Figure 8.2 JJB Sports Income Statement

Source: From JJB Sports plc Annual Report and Financial Statements 2005–2006.

⬤ JJB Sports plc

Consolidated balance sheet
As at 29 January 2006

	Note	As at 29 January 2006 £'000	As at 30 January 2005 Restated £'000
Non-current assets			
Goodwill	14	186,084	186,114
Other intangible assets	15	10,191	–
Property, plant and equipment	16	189,222	165,175
		385,497	351,289
Current assets			
Inventories	18	120,266	112,719
Trade and other receivables	19	38,738	35,792
Current asset investments	20	168,117	168,117
Cash and cash equivalents	21	34,860	29,323
		361,981	345,951
Total assets		747,478	697,240
Current liabilities			
Trade and other payables	22	(81,530)	(83,338)
Tax liabilities	23	(13,678)	(14,698)
Bank loan and loan notes	24	(168,117)	(193,067)
Short-term provisions	25	(7330)	(4969)
		(270,655)	(296,072)
Net current assets		91,326	49,879
Non-current liabilities			
Bank loan	24	(59,885)	–
Deferred tax liabilities	26	(19,785)	(19,289)
Deferred leas incentives	27	(32,560)	(24,491)
		(112,230)	(43,780)
Total liabilities		(382,885)	(339,852)
Net assets		364,593	357,388
Equity			
Share capital	28	11,538	11,533
Share premium account	30	157,219	157,219
Capital redemption reserve	31	1,069	1,069
Foreign currrency translation reserve	32	24	(21)
Retained earnings	33	194,743	187,583
Equity attributable to equity holders of the parent		364,593	357,388

Figure 8.3 JJB Sports Balance Sheet

Source: From JJB Sports plc Annual Report and Financial Statements 2005–2006.

We will come back to a lot of the information contained in these two financial statements throughout this chapter. However, if you would like to learn a bit more about the company and see the annual report for yourself why not download it from the Internet? It can be found at www.jjbcorporate.co.uk/.

INTRODUCING RATIO ANALYSIS

The purpose of financial statement analysis is to help you with your decision-making process. Such analysis can help both you and the other interested users of financial information (see Chapter 1 for details) decide on questions such as whether to lend the business money, offer credit facilities, invest in the business and buy goods. Most analysis is conducted by applying recognised techniques such as key ratios, which describe the relationship between values. Financial ratios provide a quick and relatively simple way of examining the financial health of an organisation. A ratio will express the relationship of one figure that appears on the financial statements with another (for example Gross Profit to Sales – from Chapter 7) or with another of the organisation's resources (for example the number of employees to sales). Once a ratio has been calculated it can then be compared with budgets, previous information, other businesses and industry benchmarks.

RATIO ANALYSIS

This is the calculation of ratios from a set of financial statements, which can be used to compare a business with its performance from previous years or similar businesses to provide information for decision making.

It is probably worth pointing out here that ratio analysis is not regulated like accounting practices are (see Chapter 2). Therefore, when comparing ratios you should always check the definitions that have been used – unfortunately there may be quite a few – in order to fully understand the information. Ratios cannot and should not be compared unless they are calculated on the same basis. It is therefore a good idea to state the definitions and working concepts when you do your analysis. To make things a little more straight-forward for you this book will focus on the most common types of ratios that are calculated in the sport and leisure industry.

Some of the most effective ratio analysis is relatively simple to do and is based on year on year changes. There are four other key areas to look at when assessing the financial performance and health of a company: profitability, liquidity, gearing and investment ratios. Don't worry too much about the terminology here, as it will be explained system-atically throughout the remainder of the chapter. Ultimately, however, the choice of ratios that are best to calculate will depend on the type of business and the availability of data, for example, if we are looking at a non-trading organisation such as the British Triathlon Association we will have no need to do any investment ratios, as there are no such figures!

THE STEPS OF FINANCIAL RATIO ANALYSIS

Before you cover any of the key ratios included in this chapter it is important to recognise that they are all calculated by a series of steps. It will make your life much easier and certainly less confusing if you approach all of the analysis progressively. The first of these steps will be to identify the key indicators and relationships that require some examination. It is likely that this will come out of the basic analysis that we explained in Chapter 7; for example, you may wish to examine profitability.

In order to carry out the analysis you must then consider who the target users of the analysis will be and why they need the information. As you witnessed back in Chapter 1 there are many different users that can have varied needs. For example long-term lenders of finance may be interested in the profitability and gearing of an organisation as they have a long-term interest in business viability. Suppliers, on the other hand (short term creditors), will be more interested in the liquidity of a business as they'll want to know if they are going to get their money sooner rather than later. Don't worry if you don't understand the terminology just yet as the remainder of this chapter will explain it all.

Once you are happy with the users of the analysis it will be time to do the calculations and finally the interpretations. After all the figures will be meaningless to the untrained eye. Consequently you need to be able to explain what everything means in the context of both the organisation and the wider industry. It is worth noting here that the calculation of the figures can be very easy. Once mastered you can simply get a computer spreadsheet to do things for you. The devil is in the detail though, and is where you can really impress future employers and senior management!

To help you through all of this the following sections are systematically broken down into the 'steps' we talked about earlier. You will be shown the theory behind the ratio, given the formula and then taken through the practice. For the purposes of this chapter you will find that JJB Sports is our chosen organisation but there will be plenty of opportunity for you to replicate our analysis on an organisation of your choice.

GROWTH

The growth of a business is vital if it is to continue, develop, succeed and meet the ever-changing demands of consumers in the market-place. Indeed, failure to grow might result in a loss of competitiveness, a decline in demand and in some cases eventual closure. Growth enables past trends to be examined and predictions of performance to be made in the future. Just think for a moment about how important it is in the sport and leisure industry. In English football for example, growth will be essential. A club as a whole must grow in terms of membership and fan base in order to generate increased income through ticket and merchandise sales so that it can become more competitive on the field of play. However, if a team does not grow it will not have the resources to match the larger teams in terms of player wages and squad sizes.

The best way to calculate growth is by examining year on year changes so that we can analyse how an organisation has progressed over a period of time. We can then link the analysis with other factors that appear in the annual report of an organisation such as commercial activities, sponsorship, television deals and revenue. Year on year change can be calculated with a simple formula that can be applied to the entire income statement and balance sheet. This formula is shown below and if you have a look at Figures 8.4 and 8.5 you can see what JJB Sports plc has achieved in terms of growth between 2005 and 2006. For the purposes of this analysis we have reproduced the JJB Sports plc financial statements in a spreadsheet.

$$((\text{This Year} - \text{Last Year}) / \text{Last Year}) \times 100$$

JJB Sports plc

Consolidated income statement reproduction
For the 52 weeks to 29 January 2006

		52 weeks to 29 January 2006	53 weeks to 30 January 2005 Restated	Year on Year Analysis
Continuing operations		£'000	£'000	
Revenue		**745,238**	**773,339**	**-4%**
Cost of sales		(393,075)	(402,082)	-2%
Gross profit		**352,163**	**371,257**	**-5%**
Other operating income		3,177	3,079	3%
Distribution expenses		(21,722)	(19,272)	13%
Administration expenses		(30.705)	(31,637)	-3%
Selling expenses		(268,564)	(261,321)	3%
Operating profit		**34,349**	**62,106**	**-45%**
Operating profit is stated after (charging) crediting				
Creation of provision relating to legal penalty		(1882)	(2,000)	-6%
Release of legal cost accrual		–	2,000	-100%
Net gain (loss) of disposal of property, plant and equipment		2,917	(835)	-449%
		1,035	(835)	-224%
Finance income		8,896	9,036	-2%
Finance costs		(9,498)	(8,692)	9%
Profit before taxation		**33,747**	**62,450**	**-46%**
Taxation		(3,510)	(17,287)	-80%
Profit after taxation for the period attributable to equity holders of the parent		**30,237**	**45,163**	**-33%**
Basic earnings per share	Pence	**13.10**	**19.54**	**-33%**
Diluted earnings per share	Pence	**13.10**	**19.51**	**-33%**

Figure 8.4 JJB Sports Income Statement Growth Analysis

Source: From JJB Sports plc Annual Report and Financial Statements 2005–2006.

interpreting annual reports

JJB Sports plc

Balance Sheet Growth Analysis
Consolidated balance sheet reproduction
As at 29 January 2006

	As at 29 January 2006 Restated £'000	As at 30 January 2005 Restated £'000	Year on Year Analysis
Non-current assets			
Goodwill	186,084	186,114	0%
Other tangible assets	10,191	–	–
Property, plant and equipment	189,222	165,175	15%
	385,497	351,289	10%
Current assets			
Inventories	120,266	112,719	7%
Trade and other receivables	38,738	35,792	8%
Current asset investment	168,117	168,117	0%
Cash and cash equivalents	34,860	29,323	19%
	361,981	345,951	5%
Total assets	**747,478**	**697,240**	**7%**
Current Liabilities			
Trade and other payables	(81,530)	(83,338)	–2%
Tax liabilities	(13,678)	(14,698)	–7%
Bank loan and loan notes	(168,117)	(193,067)	–13%
Short-term provisions	(7,330)	(4,969)	48%
	(270,655)	(296,072)	–9%
Net-current assets	**91,326**	**49,879**	**83%**
Non-current liabilities			
Bank loan	(59,885)	–	–
Deferred tax liabilities	(19,785)	(19,289)	3%
Deferred lease incentives	(32,560)	(24,491)	33%
	(112,230)	(43,780)	156%
Total liabilities	(382,885)	(339,852)	13%
Net assets	**364,593**	**357,388**	**2%**
Equity			
Share capital	11,538	11,538	0%
Share premium account	157,219	157,219	0%
Capital redemption reserve	1,069	1,069	0%
Foreign currency translation reserve	24	(21)	–214%
Retained earnings	194,743	187,583	4%
Equity attributable to equity holders of the parent	**364,593**	**357,388**	**2%**

Figure 8.5 JJB Sports Balance Sheet Growth Analysis

Source: From JJB Sports plc Annual Report and Financial Statements 2005–2006.

It is now a straightforward job of interpreting the year on year analysis for the income statement. First, we need to pick out the key figures. In our case these have already been noted in the basic analysis that we conducted at the beginning of this chapter. Gross profits have fallen by 5 per cent and although other operating income has increased slightly it does not compensate for the reduction in total revenue. Moreover, distribution costs have increased by 13 per cent and this will impact on the operating profit. As can be seen, operating profit fell by 45 per cent and there was a reduction of 33 per cent in profit after taxation and a reduction of more than 6 pence in basic earning per share.

Is the increase in distribution costs the key area for JJB? The year on year analysis shows that this has the biggest increase in percentage terms. However, do not be misled by percentages. Which would you prefer: 12 per cent of £1 or 5 per cent of £100,000. Hopefully you chose the latter. Similarly you must also look for absolute values when looking for key areas.

Overall JJB is showing a cause for financial concern over the previous year in line with the Chairman's comments, which were outlined in the JJB case study introduction. Further analysis of the income statement may be performed on the notes to the accounts and in the wider context of the industry.

The company is showing a small growth in total worth (2 per cent overall). The investment in fixed and current assets is improving year on year with a 7 per cent growth in total assets. In total net current assets have nearly doubled (an 83 per cent growth) although non-current liabilities have also increased, primarily due to the bank loan that has been obtained. Overall this balance sheet looks healthy as the value of the organisation's assets outweighs the liabilities.

This further work has supported some of the basic analysis that had already been undertaken and has highlighted some areas that warrant further attention. The remainder of this chapter will therefore explore these issues in more detail. However, before you move on to the profitability section have a go at the activity and try things for yourself.

ACTIVITY

Go on-line and find the annual report for a sport/leisure organisation of your choice – you could use the Financial Times link from Chapter 6. This could be a Premier League Rugby Union Club or your local cycling club. Once you have got the necessary information examine the director's and auditor's comments to begin to work out how well the organisation is performing.

Once this has been done copy the accounts into a spreadsheet and conduct the year on year analysis just like we have done for JJB. This may seem like a long-drawn-out process but the practice will help you understand the figures in much more detail. Once you've done all of that you can move on to the next section in this chapter.

PROFITABILITY RATIOS

Profitability ratios are used to review the operating performance of the business. We'll look at some key measures here including the gross profit ratio, net profit ratio, return on capital employed and a glance back at the year on year figures outlined above. Profitability is essentially a measure of the company's ability to make a profit in relation to other factors, for example, turnover. In order to create a meaningful assessment of how profitable a company is, the profit made should be considered in relation to the size of the business. We need to look at 'in relation to' because absolute figures can give a false impression. For example, which would you prefer to own: a company that made a profit of £100m or one that earned £110m? The immediate thought is 'I would prefer the one that earned £110m'. But this will change if you are told that using assets worth £200m generated the profit of £110m, whereas the company that generated the £100m did so with assets worth £80m.

To make a profit a company has to ensure that they sell goods and/or services at a higher price than the cost of producing them. However, in the sport and leisure industry there will be exceptions when determining the internal capability to generate profits due to the presence of grants, television revenue and sponsorship agreements. Remember that you can do what you like – it is you who is trying to interpret the accounts and you are doing it for your own specific reasons. Consequently, you must think of the best ways to find and compare the specific facts and trends that will best suit your purpose. However, there are some ratios that are in common usage.

Gross profit ratio

The gross profit ratio indicates to us the amount of profit that the company makes on its cost of sales (or cost of goods sold). Quite simply it shows us how much gross profit the business makes per £1 of turnover. Remember here that turnover equals sales! The gross profit (calculated as sales minus cost of sales) is therefore all of the profit that is made before other business costs have been deducted. The calculation that we shall use is

$$\text{Gross profit ratio} = \frac{\text{Gross Profit}}{\text{Turnover}} \times 100\%$$

The turnover of a business will show in absolute terms the size of the business but it does not give a feel for the efficiency and effectiveness of the business. The profitability ratios will help to do that.

	2006	2005	2004
Turnover	£745.2m	£773.3m	£771.8m
Gross profit	£352.2m	£371.3m	£425.1m
Gross profit (%)	47.3	48.0	48.7

The gross profit percentage for JJB for 2006 was 47.3 per cent. In simple terms this means that for every £1 JJB takes in sales, 47.3p of it is gross profit. However, there is not much to be gained by looking at this figure in isolation.

It can be seen that although the turnover increased from 2004 to 2005, the gross profit fell. The reasons for this can be found in the Chairman's statement in the 2005 report: 'strong competitive pressure in the clothing sector [. . .] and the clearance of excess clothing ranges and fragmented stocks'. This makes sense of the ratio: JJB had to keep prices low because of competition and also had to discount some stock to get rid of it. Both of these factors will reduce the gross profit.

Operating profit ratio

The operating profit ratio tells us the amount of operating profit per £1 of turnover that a business has been able to earn during an accounting period. This will be after all of the other business expenses such as administration and distribution costs have been deducted so it will therefore be much lower than the gross profit figure. It is advisable to use the profit figure before interest and tax are deducted. This is so that the figure that is used is a 'true' measure of operating performance and is not influenced by financing decisions (interest on loans etc.) and externalities (tax). As with the gross profit ratio we need to relate it to the turnover figure so that comparisons can be made (it is difficult to get a true feeling from absolute figures). Operating profit will be the profit before interest and taxation (PBIT).

$$\text{Operating profit ratio} = \frac{\text{PBIT}}{\text{Turnover}} \times 100\%$$

JJB Operating Profit Ratio

	2006	2005	2004
Turnover	£745.2m	£773.3m	£771.8m
PBIT	£34.3m	£62.1m	£69.1m
Operating profit (%)	4.6	8.0	8.9

If you are looking at the accounts you have to be careful to ensure that you are comparing like with like. This is illustrated in this case: JJB disposed of a part of its business in 2004 and consequently it is necessary to adjust the accounts for that to take out the discontinued business so that the remaining figures can be compared with future years.

There is a significant decrease in the operating profit percentage from 2005 to 2006. Again the reasons for this can be found in the Chief Executive's statement. The 2006 statement explains that the drop was due to accounting adjustments being made to the operating expenses to bring them in line with International Accounting Standards and also the impact of increasing the number of health clubs in the Leisure Division. It is expected that the clubs will achieve higher profits in 2007.

Return on capital employed (ROCE)

This can be tricky: there are many different views of what is meant by 'return on capital employed'. Therefore you need to be careful with how you define 'capital employed' and what 'return' it has earned! The most logical place to start is to think that if the organisation has been formed to generate profits then everything that is used in the business should be viewed as working towards that objective. This would mean that everything is viewed as being 'capital employed' and therefore the shareholders 'capital' and non-current liabilities (i.e. long-term loans) should be added together to give the total capital employed. Alternatively you can calculate the 'capital employed' by adding the non-current and current assets and subtracting the current liabilities (this will give you exactly the same figure as previously calculated).

Following on logically, the return that we should use will be the profits generated by the total capital. These profits will be before deductions for interest (this is the charge for using the loan capital and therefore shouldn't be used to reduce the profit the capital has returned), dividends (this can be viewed as being the charge for using the owners capital) and tax. This will be the operating profit.

Sometimes ROCE is referred to as the 'prime ratio'. This signifies its importance: it provides an immediate summary about management's effectiveness in generating revenue and controlling costs. The ROCE should be used as a benchmark: taking into account interest rates, risks and alternative uses, has the organisation generated a sufficient return? For example, if the current interest rate on a deposit account at a bank is 6 per cent and a company has a ROCE of 5 per cent, investors in the company would not be happy: the are getting a lower return but taking a bigger risk than bank depositors.

Return on capital employed is calculated as follows;

$$ROCE = \frac{PBIT}{CE} \times 100\%$$

JJB ROCE

	2006	**2005**	**2004**
PBIT	£34.3m	£62.1m	£69.1m
Capital employed	£476.8m	£401.2m	£462.0m
ROCE (%)	7.2	15.5	15.0

There has been a substantial drop in the ROCE from 2005 to 2006. This has been caused by the lower profits and higher capital employed. The capital employed has risen because of increased borrowings. The loans were used to finance expenditure on property, plant and equipment and the acquisition of the Slazenger golf brand.

A cautionary note: we have calculated the ROCE using the value of the capital employed in the balance sheet. As you will recall from your earlier readings, the balance sheet is a snapshot of the company at the end of the year. If the company had acquired new assets on the day before the balance sheet was compiled it would not have had time for the assets to generate a return. Obviously this can give a false view of the ROCE. Ways to overcome this problem are to reconstruct the capital employed or to take the average of the capital at the beginning and end of the year. However, looking at the long-run trend of the ratio can lessen the distortion.

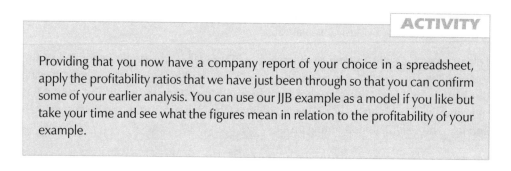

Turnover/capital employed

This ratio will show how 'hard' the business has been working in relation to the size of the assets used (as measured by the capital employed).

JJB Turnover/Capital employed

	2006	2005	2004
Turnover	£745.2m	£773.3m	£771.8m
Capital employed	£476.8m	£401.2m	£462.0m
Turnover/capital employed	1.56	1.93	1.67

Secondary analysis – a deeper analysis!

Hopefully you will have realised that we have used some figures several times. What can we gain by an analysis based on just a few figures? Hopefully quite a lot! The analysis we have undertaken so far could enable you to spot a company's strategy or how its operations differ from those of its competitors. We said that ROCE was often referred to as the prime ratio; as such the 'prime' can be split into secondary elements. Here is the formula for ROCE again:

$$ROCE = \frac{PBIT}{CE} \times 100\%$$

Mathematical dexterity will allow us to play about with that equation to show that:

$$\frac{PBIT}{CE} = \frac{PBIT}{Turnover} \times \frac{Turnover}{CE}$$

Therefore we can see that:

$$ROCE = \frac{PBIT}{Turnover} \times \frac{Turnover}{CE}$$

So, we can see that the return a business generates is a function of its profit margin and how hard it works its assets. Two companies could each have a ROCE of 8 per cent but one could generate it by 4×2 and the other could get there by 2×4. This would imply two different strategies: one company operates with a high margin but low utilisation of its assets but the other company has lower margins but generates them more often.

LIQUIDITY RATIOS

As you should have picked up from the cash flow forecast section in the previous chapter, cash is the lifeblood of any business. A business must pay its debts as they fall due or risk financial failure (remember the Leeds United case study). The liquidity ratios are a tool for measuring the solvency and financial stability of a business so that we can assess how effectively it has managed its working capital. Liquidity is therefore about the ability of a business to generate sufficient cash to meet its liabilities as they fall due. You should also note that much like the fact that profit is different to cash, profitability should not be confused with liquidity here. A company could be very profitable but not liquid and will therefore not be able to meet its immediate obligations. There are two principle ratios that you will need to be aware of here; the current ratio and quick ratio. Liquidity ratios are normally expressed as real ratios i.e. x:1 rather than z per cent.

LIQUIDITY

Liquidity measures the ability of a company to access enough cash to meet its liabilities as they fall due.

The current ratio

The current ratio compares current assets with current liabilities. This will help to discover whether the company has enough resources to meet its immediate financial requirements. Many analysts recommend that a company should have a ratio of at least 1:1, indicating that it has £1 of resource to cover £1 of liability. However this is too general: it is like saying that every football team should play in a 4-4-2 formation. The industry and many other factors will determine the liquidity profile of a company. For example a supermarket will have the ability to generate cash a lot quicker than a clothing manufacturer: the supermarket has shelves full of goods that will become cash as soon as a shopper takes them to the check-out whereas the clothing manufacturer will have to wait for its debtor to pay on credit terms.

You may think that it is good to have a lot of current assets but you should also consider the fact that you can have too many! It is not good management if you have too much stock and cash floating about in the business: they should be working not floating!

$$\text{Current Ration} = \frac{\text{Current Assets}}{\text{Current Liabilities}}$$

JJB Current Ratio

	2006	2005	2004
Current assets £m	362.0	346.0	391.3
Current liabilities £m	270.7	296.1	271.5
Current ratio	1.34:1	1.17:1	1.44:1

The ratio shows that JJB has sufficient current assets to cover its current liabilities. The table shows that the ratio fluctuates. What could be the reason for this? The first thing to consider is the fact that JJB is a retailer: have there been changes in the amount of inventory (stock) it holds? Has JJB opened more shops and therefore needs to have goods in these shops? Is there inventory that it can't sell? What about the liabilities: has JJB stopped paying its creditors and therefore the amounts it owes have escalated? When you are doing your own analysis you might get answers to these questions from the annual report. If not you will have to think! In the case of JJB the increase in liabilities was due to a long-term loan becoming payable within the next period.

The quick ratio (acid test)

The quick ratio (or acid test) is similar to the current ratio with the exception that inventory (stock) is excluded from the current assets because the inventory may not be 'liquid'. In other words the inventory is excluded because it may take a while before the inventory can be sold and then there may be a further wait until it is paid for. The circumstances will depend on the type of company: the trading cycle for a supermarket is very different to that of a leisure centre for example. However, because most sport and leisure organisations exist to provide a service to the public, not to sell stock, it is probable that very little stock will be held.

The quick ratio is therefore a stringent way of testing whether the organisation has the ability to pay debtors if they demanded their cash immediately. Again, it is more insightful to look for trends and examine the particular circumstances of an organisation than to look for a golden number. Obviously an organisation with a quick ratio of less than one to one would have to stall for time if the boys with the baseball bats called round to demand that the current liabilities be paid immediately.

$$\text{Quick Ratio} = \frac{\text{Current Assets} - \text{Inventory}}{\text{Current Liabilities}}$$

JJB Quick Ratio

	2006	2005	2004
Current assets £m	362.0	346.0	391.3
Inventory £m	120.3	112.7	128.1
Current liabilities £m	270.7	296.1	271.5
Quick ratio	0.89	0.79	0.97

JJB is obviously happy to operate with a quick ratio of less than 1:1. This is not surprising: it is a retailer and the vast majority of the sales will be cash.

It is important for any financial manager to track these ratios as any unexplained movements from one annual report to the next can encourage observers to draw their conclusions about the liquidity position and creditworthiness of the company.

DEFENSIVE POSITION RATIOS (LONG-TERM SOLVENCY)

Two key ratios are the debt ratio and the gearing ratio. For professional team sports these may be two of the most useful methods in deciding how well a company is performing because they measure the relationship between capital (equity) and long-term debt. Again think back to the Leeds United case study – it is fair to say that they had a great deal of long-term debt and that this got them into a poor financial situation. These ratios allow us to examine the company's financial structure. Investors and other users of accounting information can use defensive position ratios to assess the level of financial risk – they can estimate when (or if) they are likely to get their money back. Consequently these ratios are a more long-term financial measure of the risk taken by an organisation in regards to the amount of money it has borrowed. In general the lower the level of borrowings the business has, the healthier a position it is in to withstand poor trading conditions. Interest payments on loans and overdrafts have to be paid irrespective of turnover and ticket sales.

The debt ratio

The debt ratio shows the extent to which creditors have power over an organisation. A high ratio indicates that the creditors are funding most of the firm's assets. Consequently, if the creditors decide that they want repaying, the organisation may have to sell off some of its assets to raise the cash needed to pay off the creditors. In terms of the sport and leisure industry this may mean, for example, a football club having to sell some of its players to pay creditors when they demand their cash. A debt ratio of 50 per cent is considered a safe limit whereas a debt ratio exceeding 75 per cent is a cause for concern. However, the specific context of the organisation must be taken into account. The debt ratio is calculated by the following formula:

$$\text{Debt Ratio} = \frac{\text{Total Debt}}{\text{Total Assets}} \times 100\%$$

The total debt will be equal to current liabilities plus long-term liabilities (loans).

JJB Debt Ratio

	2006	2005	2004
Current liabilities	£270.7m	£296.1m	£271.5m
Long-term liabilities	£59.9m	0	£84.8m
Total assets	£747.5m	£697.2m	£733.4m
Debt ratio (%)	44.2	42.5	48.6

Although JJB has changed the profile of its debts, the overall structure has kept the debt ratio below 50 per cent.

The gearing ratio

The gearing ratio can be used to measure how the organisation is financed. Gearing refers to how much of the capital is made up of debt finance. The financial structure is a very important aspect of financial management: get it right and there are many benefits but getting it wrong can be disastrous. Debt finance is attractive to organisations because it is cheap and there are tax benefits (interest payments are allowable tax expenses) but the interest payments (and the capital of the loan) are contractual obligations. Interest and the loan itself have to be paid irrespective of how well the organisation is performing. If there is a downturn in the fortunes of the company it will still have to meet these obligations. Shareholders' dividend payments are not contractual: they are paid if there is a profit after all other obligations have been met. In a company that has a lot of debt finance, shareholders are risking that there will still be enough profit left after the associated loan payments to pay them a dividend. The same idea applies to other investors: if a highly geared company is trying to raise additional capital new investors could view it as a bad risk. Simply put, gearing shows us how much of an organisation is financed by loans.

SHARES

Shares are parts of the business that are issued to people in return for cash. It is only when the shares are initially issued that the company receives any cash. Any other sale of the shares is between private individuals (or institutions).

SHAREHOLDER

A shareholder is one of the owners of the shares in a company. Collectively the shareholders own the whole company.

DIVIDENDS

Dividends are amounts of money paid to shareholders from profits earned by a company. It is usual for the total payment to be paid in two instalments: an interim payment part way through the year and then the final payments at the year end. Dividend payments are discretionary: they do not have to be paid.

The formula for the gearing ratio is shown below;

$$\text{Gearing Ratio} = \frac{\text{Long-term Liabilities}}{\text{Capital Employed}} \times 100\%$$

JJB Gearing Ratio

	2006	**2005**	**2004**
Long-term liabilities	£59.9m	0	£84.8m
Capital employed	£476.8m	£401.2m	£462.0m
ROCE (%)	12.6	N/A	18.4

These figures give the impression that JJB takes a conservative view of gearing and appears to have the capacity to raise more debt finance if it needed extra capital to expand its operations. The anomaly of 2005 is explained in the notes accompanying the financial statements: 'In June 2005, JJB's existing £100 million committed revolving bank credit facility expired. This was replaced by a new 5 year £60 million revolving bank credit facility which commenced in June 2005'. However the amount of short-term debt needs to be taken into account to get a more holistic view (see the debt ratio).

Interest cover

This ratio will show the relationship between the profit for the period and the interest that has to be paid. This ratio will give a quick insight into the ability of an organisation to meet its current, and potentially new, repayments. It is interest to present and potential lenders of finance, and also to shareholders (because their profits are not earned until all obligations have been met).

JJB Interest Cover

	2006	**2005**	**2004**
Interest cover	3.62	7.15	7.06

The interest cover has fallen significantly in 2006. Again the reasons are given in the Annual Report: increased borrowings to finance higher expenditure on intangible assets, property, plant and equipment. Without the underlying strategy as detailed in the Annual Report the shareholders could become worried: there is still a further call (tax) on the profits before the surplus is theirs.

INVESTMENT RATIOS

Existing and potential investors want to see what the benefits are, or will be, for investing in a company, i.e. becoming a shareholder. Some of the ratios that you have used so far will have given you an insight into the profitability, liquidity and defensive position of a business and these should enable to you gain an insight into the effectiveness of the organisation's management.

However, investment ratios allow us to quickly obtain an overview of the results of the organisation from the perspective of an investment, i.e. the rewards due to the shareholders. Existing and potential shareholders will want to see if they are getting a good return on their investment. Obviously shareholder ratios can only be applied to organisations that have shareholders: remember some organisations may be not-for-profit, or clubs and societies.

Investor ratios are calculated for many organisations on a daily basis. You can easily access them by looking at the financial pages of 'up-market' newspapers. They are usually towards the back of the paper: after Page 3 but before the sport!

Earnings per share

This, as the name implies, shows the earnings that are attributable to each share. The earnings that each share is entitled to will be the net profit (that is profit after all deductions, including payments to preference shareholders) divided by the number of 'ordinary' shares.

The 'earnings per share' figure when viewed in isolation is totally meaningless to any investor. If the earnings per share for Company A is 25p and for Company B it is 80p, what is the significance of that information? Answer: absolutely none! In fact the answer provides the reason: they are absolute values. To get any meaning we need to compare them to something, and that something is the price of the share. This is done by the 'price/earnings' ratio.

Price/earnings ratio

The price/earnings ratio (P/E) relates the earnings per share to the price of the share: it therefore looks at the size of the investment (as measured by the current trading price of a share in the company) and the reward paid to the holder of that share.

A high P/E ratio signals that investors have a high expectation of the future prospects of the company. This is because they are willing to pay a high price for the share. The ratio tells us how many years it will take (based on today's trading price for a share) for a shareholder's return from the company to equal the price paid for the share.

What is an acceptable level of return? The only possible answer to that question is: 'it depends'. There are many factors to consider before anyone can offer their opinion (and it can only ever be their own personal opinion!) about what is an acceptable level of return. Factors for consideration are: the risk associated with that specific organisation, the risk associated with the business sector that the organisation operates in, alternative investments available, personal preference and beliefs, personal attitude to risk. Do we all support the same football team? Does everyone bet on the same horse in a race? Why not? Do all investors buy the same shares? Does the price of shares stay at the same price? Why not?

The reward for taking a bigger risk is a bigger return. That is why some finance companies will lend money to struggling companies: they will charge them a high interest! The quantification of risk (can it ever be quantified if there is so much personal belief involved?) is a 'science' in its own right but the market-place will always find a seller when the buyer's needs are big enough!

This is probably the most important investment ratio as it works out the average amount of profits earned per ordinary share issued. Any profit retained in the company to help it grow will still belong to the shareholders and as such any dividend that they receive will only be part of the return of their investment.

Dividend per share

This shows the amount of profit allocated to pay dividends. Many companies will only make a certain amount of money available to shareholders by way of dividend, as they will want to use some of the profits for other things such as reinvestment in equipment and relocations etc. Therefore the dividend per share gives you a feel for the short-term return on an investment.

Overall return

The long-term return will include the annual dividend payments and 'capital' growth. For example, if you bought a share today for £2 and the company paid dividends of 15p and 23p in the next two years and at the end of the second year the share price was £2.40, your total gain would be 40p plus 15p plus 23p. That would give you a total gain of 78p (a total growth of 39 per cent on your initial investment over two years). However, the 40p capital gain would only be realised if you sold the share. Therefore you must constantly review the prospects for the company and ask: 'do I want to continue my investment or can I get a better return elsewhere?'

The dividend policy of an organisation can have an impact on the type of investor it attracts. Some investors may want regular substantial cash flows and will therefore like a company that pays high dividends while other investors may be in for the long haul and prefer the company to retain profits (as opposed to paying them out in dividends) and use them to fund expansion and future growth.

Wealth warning

Investing can seriously damage your wealth. Investments can go down. Before you invest in anything make sure that you have done the preparatory research. Also, remember that many people have got small fortunes by investing in football clubs: unfortunately they had large fortunes before they invested!

ACTIVITY

1   If you haven't done so already follow the investment ratios and apply them to your company. What do your results tell you?
2   Having done all of the analysis what is your assessment of the organisation's current financial position and performance? Remember to couple your analysis with the director's report and the general figures contained in the income statement and balance sheet.

RATIO ANALYSIS AND ITS LIMITS

As with any measurement tool there will be limitations. Ratio analysis is no different. If we agree that the level and choice of analysis depends on the user and the availability of useful data then we agree that there will be differences in the findings. For example, with an organisation such as the British Triathlon Association not all of the ratios would be applicable. However, there are a few more limitations to ratio analysis that you should be aware of. We have alluded to some of these already but it is worth recapping:

- There are no universally agreed definitions for the formulas and terminology used. Ratios based on alternative meanings should not be compared! Consequently, always state the definitions you are using whenever you prepare any analysis.
- Some data may not be available so you may have to use less precise material.
- Ideally you should do some trend analysis but again this information may not always be available or comparable.
- Comparisons with other companies in the industry may be difficult if their data is not published – how do you really know how you are doing?
- The sport and leisure industry is always in a period of rapid change and therefore some analysis is out of date before it is completed because of the changes in the operating environment!
- Non-financial factors are not considered in ratio analysis (this is why you should always refer to the director's reports).

Notwithstanding such limitations, ratio analysis – when used in conjunction with a full range of material – is a very useful management tool and one that we believe you should be competent in. You should be aware that ratios should not just be viewed as 'facts' but as a method of indicating where further research may be required. The real reasons for financial position and performance need to be communicated by you (as managers) in order to make effective business decisions.

SUMMARY

This chapter has shown you how to dissect annual reports in a meaningful and trustworthy manner. Ratio analysis is fundamental in your own personal development as managers and will help inform you of problems, potential issues and successful ideas. However, access to the appropriate data is integral to calculating the right things and the results can be widely used by a variety of user groups (as outlined in Chapter 1). We have only shown you the common ratios that are used in the context of sport and leisure organisations so if you gain employment outside this sector you should familiarise yourselves with the specific industry requirements.

In order to make meaningful comparisons you need to interpret the industry trends and examine the director's report. This will enable you to make a well-rounded response to questions from an organisation. Despite the drawbacks outlined in the final section of this chapter you should realise what an important tool ratios are!

Although annual reports can be very useful to us as users of financial statements, the main problem with them is the sheer volume of information contained within them – if you accessed the JJB report as suggested you'll know exactly what we mean here! In order to make sensible use of the figures you need to organise them in a logical way. Several of the techniques covered in this chapter go way beyond the basic analysis we covered in Chapter 6, however in ratio analysis we have a framework that we can apply to draw some meaningful conclusions about the financial health of an organisation.

ADDITIONAL CASE STUDY

Why not go back to the Arena Leisure case study that we asked you to look at in Chapters 1 and 7 and conduct the same analysis as we have done for JJB? If you haven't already done so get on-line and download their annual report. It can be found at www.arenaleisureplc.com.

QUESTIONS FOR REVIEW

1   What is the purpose of ratio analysis?
2   What are the five key measures for a business?
3   What is ROCE?
4   What is liquidity and how can it be measured?
5   List and explain three limitations of ratio analysis.

1   Ratio analysis is used to measure and compare the performance and financial health of an organisation from year to year or against similar companies.

2   The five key areas are: growth, profitability, defensive position, liquidity and investment ratios.

3   ROCE is the return on capital employed and therefore shows the 'reward' that has been gained by utilising the capital in the organisation.

4   Liquidity is a measure of how quickly an organisation could cover its immediate liabilities if they demanded payment. It can be measured by the current ratio and the quick (acid test) ratio.

5   Hopefully you covered three of the points we discussed earlier in the chapter. These can be drawn from the following list:

▣   There are no universally agreed definitions for the formulas and terminology used.

▣   Some data may not be available so you may have to use less precise material.

▣   Comparisons with other companies in the industry may be difficult if their data is not published – how do you really know how you are doing?

▣   The sport and leisure industry is always in a period of rapid change and therefore some analysis is out of date before it is completed because of the changes in the operating environment!

▣   Non-financial factors are not considered in ratio analysis.

GLOSSARY OF TERMS

Below you will find all of the key terms that are covered throughout this book in one place – this will help you understand the terminology throughout instead of having to keep flicking back through previous chapters.

Account: a record that is kept as part of an accounting system. It will be a record of the transactions and will be recorded in monetary values.

Accounting: is about identifying, collecting, measuring, recording, summarising and communicating financial information.

Accounting equation: Assets – Liabilities = Capital.

Accruals: the accruals basis of accounting requires the non-cash effects of transactions and other events to be reflected in the financial statements for the accounting period in which they occur and not in the period when the cash is paid or received.

Annual Report: the financial statements, directors' report, auditor's report and other information published by an organisation on an annual basis.

Asset disposal: the term used to explain the sale of fixed assets when they reach the end of their useful life.

Assets: these are items or resources that have a value to the business and things that are used by the business and for the business. Normally we will classify assets as either fixed or current. The basic difference being that a fixed asset is something that the business intends to keep and use for some time whereas a current asset is held for the business to convert into cash during trading. Some good examples here are business premises, motor vehicles that are fixed assets and stock and cash, which are current assets.

Bad debts: a debt that the company has decided is unlikely to be paid.

Balance sheet: a list of all of the assets owned by a business and all of the liabilities owed by a business at a specific point in time. It is often referred to as a 'snapshot' of the financial position of the business at a specific moment in time (normally the end of the financial year).

Borrowings: amounts of finance that the company has borrowed from lenders in the form of overdraft facilities and loans etc.

Business entity concept: dictates that a line is drawn between the business and its owner(s): the business and its owner(s) are two separate entities.

Capital: is generally considered to be the owners' stake in the business and may also be called equity. To take this a step further it is also the excess of assets over liabilities.

Cash flow statement: a financial summary of all of the cash receipts and payments over an accounting period.

Closing stock (inventory): the value of stock (inventory) that is held at the end of a period.

Consistency concept: similar items within a single set of accounts should be given similar accounting treatment and the same treatment should be applied from one accounting period to the next for similar items so that one year's results are comparable to the next.

Corporate statement: a statement of an organisation's goal for the financial period to use when considering how they have performed over the financial period.

Cost of sales: the cost of goods sold during the period. For a retailer this will be calculated as Opening stock + Purchases – Closing Stock. For a manufacturing company it will include all of the production costs.

Creditor: an entity or person to whom money is owed.

Debtor: an entity or person who owes money to the business.

Depreciation: a notional charge made in the accounts to represent the use of an asset. It also serves to reduce the value of an asset in the balance sheet.

Dividends: amounts of money paid to shareholders from profits earned by a company. It is usual for the total payment to be paid in two instalments: an interim payment part way through the year and then the final payments at the year end. Dividend payments are discretionary: they do not have to be paid.

Double-entry rule/bookkeeping: the principle that every financial transaction involves two items.

Dual aspect concept: each transaction conducted by a business will affect two items within the business.

Expenses: the reverse of income! All money spent in relation to the company's activities.

Financial accounting: the preparation of information for external use, and is mainly concerned with reporting on past events

Financial statements: the complete set of accounts. This will include the balance sheet (this shows the organisation's assets and liabilities), income statement (the profit and loss account) and the cash flow statement. Also included will be notes on the accounting policies used and significant activities.

Going concern: the information presented in the financial statements is prepared on the basis that the organisation will continue to operate for the foreseeable future.

Gross profit: sales income minus the direct cost of the goods or services sold to customers i.e. sales minus cost of sales.

Historical cost concept: dictates that the value of items that a business owns must be based on their original cost and must not be adjusted for any subsequent changes in price or value.

Income: all money that is received or receivable.

Income statement (P&L account): a statement showing the profits (or losses) recognised during a period. The profit is calculated by deducting expenditure (including charges for capital maintenance) from income.

Intangible fixed asset: a fixed asset that has no physical existence. Examples are goodwill, patents and trademarks.

Liabilities: amounts owed by the business to people other than the owner. Normally we will see liabilities classified as either payable within one year (current liabilities) e.g. bank overdrafts, supplier accounts, or payable after one year (non-current liabilities) e.g. longer-term bank loans.

Limited company: a company registered with the Registrar of Companies whose shareholders enjoy limited liability.

Limited liability: legal protection given to the shareholders of a limited company. When a company cannot pay its debts the shareholders will not be liable to contribute more than their initial investment towards the overall debt.

Liquidation: this is quite simply the process by which a limited company ceases to exist. It is a legal status rather than a financial position.

Liquidity: the term used to describe the ability of an organisation to generate sufficient cash to meet its liabilities as they fall due.

Loans: money borrowed or lent. In an organisation's accounts it normally means amounts borrowed, as amounts lent are usually called investments. Loans are normally arranged by banks and will be noted as long-term (non-current) liabilities.

Management accounting: is about providing information that is primarily focused on the needs of management and will therefore additionally look to the future and will cover planning and control aspects. Management accounting is not a statutory requirement.

Materiality concept: only items of significance are included in the financial statements. An item is significant if its omission or misrepresentation could influence the economic decisions of those using the financial statements.

Money measurement concept: only items of monetary value can be recorded in the financial statements.

Nominal ledger (T account): an accounting record, which summarises the financial affairs of a business containing details of assets, liabilities, incomes and expenditures.

Opening stock (inventory): the value of stock that is held at the beginning of a financial period.

Operating profit: the profit of a business which is generated from its ordinary activities.

Overdraft: the amount owing to a bank on a current account.

Partnerships: two or more people enter into business together. The liability will be shared between the owners and at least one of them will have unlimited liability for the debts they may incur.

Patent: the exclusive right to use an invention. The value of a patent may be carried in the accounts as an intangible asset.

Profit: a positive residue between sales income and total expenses for a financial period.

Profit and loss account (income statement): a statement showing the profits (or losses) recognised during a period. The profit is calculated by deducting expenditure (including charges for capital maintenance) from income.

Prudence concept: states that revenue and profits are not anticipated but are recognised only when they are realised.

Public company (plc): a plc has shares, which can be purchased by anyone on the stock exchange. Ownership is therefore open to anyone who wants to buy shares. Plcs have legal requirements in that they have to produce annual reports and accounts and file them with Companies House. They must have two directors.

Residual value: the value of a fixed asset after it has been fully depreciated. It may often be the same as an item's scrap value.

Return on capital employed (ROCE): the ratio of profit before interest and tax to capital used to earn the profits. It shows the 'reward' that has been gained by utilising the capital in the organisation.

Sales: the amount shown on the income statement indicating the value of goods and services supplied to customers.

Shareholder: someone who owns shares in an organisation. Collectively all of the shareholders own the organisation concerned.

Sole trader: one person owns the business. There is no legal separation of identity between the business and the owner.

Stock: items held by a company for sale, conversion to a product for sale or consumption in production. Now also referred to as 'Inventory'.

Tangible fixed asset: a fixed asset that has a physical existence. Examples are vehicles, furniture, buildings and equipment.

Trademark: a word or symbol that identifies specific goods or specific services. The value of a trademark may be carried in the accounts as an intangible asset.

Trial balance: a list of nominal ledger ('T') account balances. It is used primarily as a measure to see if credit balances equal debit balances. Ultimately it will offer some reassurance that the double entry rule has been applied correctly.

Turnover: another term for the sales figure on an organisation's income statement.

Unlimited liability: the opposite of limited liability! At least one of the shareholders (be it a sole trader or partnership) will be liable for the total debt their company incurs.

Zyzzyva: a tropical American weevil. You will now be able to impress your family and friends by your knowledge of accounting and the last word in the dictionary!

INDEX